George Saintsbury

Political Pamphlets

George Saintsbury

Political Pamphlets

ISBN/EAN: 9783337079505

Printed in Europe, USA, Canada, Australia, Japan

Cover: Foto ©Suzi / pixelio.de

More available books at **www.hansebooks.com**

POLITICAL PAMPHLETS

EDITED BY

GEORGE SAINTSBURY

NEW YORK

MACMILLAN & CO.

1892

CONTENTS

PAGE

I. LETTER TO A DISSENTER. (By George Savile, Marquess of Halifax) 1

II. THE SHORTEST WAY WITH THE DISSENTERS. (By Daniel Defoe) 23

III. THE DRAPIER'S LETTERS. (By Jonathan Swift) To the Tradesmen, Shop-Keepers, Farmers, and Common-People in general, of the Kingdom of Ireland; concerning the Brass half-pence coined by Mr. Wood . . . . . 47.

A Letter to Mr. Harding the Printer, upon occasion of a Paragraph in his News-Paper of August 1, 1724, relating to Mr. Wood's Half-pence 64

IV. SECOND LETTER ON A REGICIDE PEACE. (By the Right Honourable Edmund Burke) . . 81

V. PETER PLYMLEY'S LETTERS. (By Sydney Smith) 133

VI. LETTER TO THE JOURNEYMEN AND LABOURERS OF ENGLAND, WALES, SCOTLAND, AND IRELAND. LETTER TO JACK HARROW. (By William Cobbett) 182

VII. FIRST LETTER OF MALACHI MALAGROWTHER. (By Sir Walter Scott) 249

INTRODUCTION

It is sometimes thought, and very often said, that political writing, after its special day is done, becomes more dead than any other kind of literature, or even journalism. I do not know whether my own judgment is perverted by the fact of a special devotion to the business, but it certainly seems to me that both the thought and the saying are mistakes. Indeed, a rough-and-ready refutation of them is supplied by the fact that, in no few cases, political pieces have entered into the generally admitted stock of the best literary things. If they are little read, can we honestly say that other things in the same rank are read much more ? And is there not the further plea, by no means contradictory, nor even merely alternative, that the best examples of them are, as a rule, merged in huge collected 'Works,' or, in the case of authors who have not attained to that dignity, simply inaccessible to the general? At any rate my publishers have consented to let me try the experiment of gathering certain famous things of the sort in this volume, and the public must decide.

I do not begin very early, partly because examples of the Elizabethan political pamphlet, or what supplied its place, will be given in another volume of the series exclusively devoted to the pamphlet literature of the reigns of Eliza and our James, partly for a still better reason presently to be explained. On the other hand, though another special volume is devoted to Defoe, the immortal *Shortest Way with the Dissenters* is separated from the rest of his work, and given here. Most of the contents, however, represent authors not otherwise represented in the series, and though very well known indeed by name, less read than quoted. The suitableness of the political pamphlet, both by size and self-containedness, for such a volume as this, needs no justification except that which it, like everything else, must receive, by being put to the proof of reading.

There is no difficulty in showing, with at least sufficient critical exactness, why it is not possible or not desirable to select examples from very early periods even of strictly modern history. The causes are in part the same as those which delayed the production of really capital political verse (which has been treated in another volume), but they are not wholly the same. The Martin Marprelate pamphlets are strictly political ; so are many things earlier, later, and contemporary with them, by hands known and unknown, great and small, skilled and unskilled ; so are some even in the work of so great a man as Bacon. But very many things were wanting to secure the conditions necessary to the perfect pamphlet. There was not the political freedom ; there was not the public ; there was not the immediate object; there was not, last and most of all, the style. Political utterances under a more or less despotic, or, as the modern euphemism goes, ' personal ' government, were almost necessarily those of a retained advocate, who expected his immediate reward, on the one hand ; or of a rebel, who stood to make his account with office if he succeeded, or with savage punishment if he failed, on the other. A distant prospect of impeachment, of the loss of ears, hands, or life if the tide turns, is a stimulant to violence rather than to vigour. I do not think, however, that this is the most important factor in the problem. Parliamentary government, with a limited franchise of tolerably intelligent voters, a party system, and newspapers comparatively unde-

veloped, may not suit an ideally perfect *politeia*, but
it is the very hotbed in which to nourish the pamphlet.   There is also a style, as there is a time, for
all things; and no style could be so well suited for
the pamphlet as the balanced, measured, pointed,
and polished style which Dryden and Tillotson and
Temple brought in during the third quarter of the
seventeenth century, and which did not go out of
fashion till the second quarter of the nineteenth.
We have indeed seen pamphlets proper exercising
considerable influence in quite recent times; but
in no instance that I can remember has this been
due to any literary merits, and I doubt whether
even the bare fact will be soon or often renewed
in our days.   The written word—the written word of
condensed, strengthened, spirited literature—has lost
much, if not all, of its force with an enormously increased electorate, and a bewildering multiplicity of
print and speech of all kinds.

Whatever justice these reasonings may have or
may lack, the facts speak for themselves, as facts
intelligently regarded have a habit of doing.   The
first pamphlets proper of great literary merit and
great political influence are those of Halifax in the
first movement of real party struggle during the reign

of Charles the Second ; the last which unite the same requisites are those of Scott on the eve of the first Reform Bill. The leaflet and circular war of the anti-Corn Law League must be ruled out as much as Mr. Gladstone's *Bulgarian Horrors.*

This leaves us a period of almost exactly a hundred and fifty years, during which the kind, whether in good or bad examples, was of constant influence, while its best instances enriched literature with permanent masterpieces in little. I do not think that any moderately instructed person will find much difficulty in comprehending the specimens here given. I am sure that no moderately intelligent one will fail, with a very little trouble, to take delight in them. I do not know whether an artful generaliser could get anything out of the circumstances in which the best of them grew ; I should say myself that nothing more than the system of government, the conditions of the electorate and the legislature, and the existence from time to time of a superheated state in political feeling, can or need be collected. In some respects, to my own taste, the first of these examples is also the best. To Halifax full justice has never been done, for we have had no capable historian of the late seventeenth century but Macaulay, and Halifax's defect of fervour as a Jacobite was more than made up to Macaulay by his defect of fervour as a Williamite. As for the moderns, I have myself more than once failed to induce editors of 'series' to give Halifax a place. Yet Macaulay himself has been fairer to the great Trimmer than to most persons with whom he was not in full sympathy. The weakness of Halifax's position is indeed obvious. When you run first to one side of the boat and then to the other, you have ten chances of sinking to one of trimming her. To hold fast to one party only, and to keep that from extremes, is the only secret, and it is no great disgrace to Halifax, that in the very infancy of the party and parliamentary system, he did not perceive it. But this hardly interferes at all with the excellence of his pamphlets. The polished style, the admirable sense, the subdued and yet ever present wit, the avoidance of excessive cleverness (the one thing that the average Briton will not stand), the constant eye on the object, are unmistakable. They are nearly as forcible as Dryden's political and controversial prefaces, which are pamphlets themselves in their way, and they excel them in knowledge of affairs, in urbanity, in adaptation to the special purpose. In all these points they resemble more than anything else the pamphlets of Paul Louis Courier, and there can be no higher praise than this.

No age in English history was more fertile in pamphlets than the reigns of William and of Anne. Some men of real distinction occasionally contributed to them, and others (such as Ferguson and Maynwaring) obtained such literary notoriety as they possess by their means. The total volume of the kind produced during the quarter of a century between the Revolution and the accession of George the First would probably fill a considerable library. But the examples which really deserve exhumation are very few, and I doubt whether any can pretend to vie with the masterpieces of Defoe and Swift. Both these great writers were accomplished practitioners in the art, and the characteristics of both lent themselves with peculiar yet strangely different readiness to the work. They addressed, indeed, different sections of what was even then the electorate. Defoe's unpolished realism and his exact adaptation of tone, thought, taste, and fancy to the measure of the common Englishman were what chiefly gave him a hearing. Swift aimed and flew higher, but also did not miss the lower mark. No one has ever doubted that Johnson's depreciation of *The Conduct of the Allies* was half special perversity (for he was always unjust to Swift), half mere humorous paradox. For there was much more of this in the doctor's utterances than his admirers, either in his own day or since, have always recognised, or have sometimes been qualified by Providence to recognise. As for the *Drapier's Letters* I can never myself admire them enough, and they seem to me to have been on the whole under- rather than over- valued by posterity.

The 'Great Walpolian Battle' and the attacks on Bute and other favourite ministers were very fertile in the pamphlet, but already there were certain signs of alteration in its character. Pulteney and Walpole's other adversaries had already glimmerings of the newspaper proper, that is to say, of the continual dropping fire rather than the single heavy broadside ; to adopt a better metaphor still, of a regimental and professional soldiery rather than of single volunteer champions. The *Letters of Junius*, which for some time past have been gradually dropping from their former somewhat undue pride of place (gained and kept as much by the factitious mystery of their origin as by anything else) to a station more justly warranted, are no doubt themselves pamphlets of a kind ; but they are separated from pamphlets proper not less by their contents than by their form and continuity. The real difference is this, that the pamphlet, though often if not always personal enough, should always and generally does affect at least to discuss a general question of principle or policy, whereas Junius is always personal first, and very generally last also. On the other hand, Burke, whether his productions be called Speeches or Letters, Thoughts or Reflections, is always a pamphleteer in heart and soul, in form and matter. If the resemblance of his pamphlets to speeches gives the force and fire, it is certain that the resemblance of his speeches to pamphlets accounts for that 'dinner-bell' effect of his which has puzzled some people and shocked others. Burke always argued the point, if he only argued one side of it, and it is the special as it is the saving grace of the pamphlet that it must, or at least should, be an argument, and not merely an invective or an innuendo, a sermon or a lampoon.

Sydney Smith belonged both to the old school and the new. He was both pamphleteer and journalist; but he kept the form and even to some extent the style of his pamphlets and his articles well apart. I may seem likely to have some difficulty in admitting the claim of Cobbett after disallowing that of Junius under the definition just given, but I have no very great fear of being unable to making it good. Much as Cobbett disliked persons, and crotchety as he was in his dislikes, they were always dislikes of principle in the bottom. The singular Tory-Radicalism which Cobbett exhibited, and which has made some rank him unduly low, was no doubt partly due to accidents of birth and education, and to narrowness of intellectual form. But boroughmongering after all was a Whig rather than a Tory institution, and Cobbett's hatred of it, as well as that desire for the maintenance of a kind of manufacturing yeomanry (not wholly different from the later ideal of Mr. William Morris,) which was his other guiding principle throughout, was by no means alien from pure Toryism. His work in relation to Reform, moreover, is unmistakable —as unmistakable as is that of Sydney Smith, who precedes him here, with regard to Catholic Emancipation. I should have voted and written against both these things had I lived then; but this does not make me enjoy Cobbett or Sydney any the less.

As for the latest example I have selected, it is a crucial one. The *Letters of Malachi Malagrowther* come from a man who is not often rated high as a political thinker, even by those who sympathise

with his political views. But here as elsewhere
the politician, no less than the poet, the critic,
the historian, bears the penalty of the pre-eminent
greatness of the novelist. Nothing is more uncritical
than to regard Scott as a mere sentimentalist in politics, and I cannot think that any competent judge
can do so after reading *Malagrowther*, even after
reading Scott's own Diary and letters on the subject.
As he there explains, he was not greatly carried, as a
rule, to interest himself in the details of politics. As
both Lockhart and he admit, he might not have been
so interested even at this juncture had it not been
for the chagrin at his own misfortunes, which, nobly
and stoically repressed as it was, required some issue.
But his general principle on this occasion was clear ;
it can be thoroughly apprehended and appreciated
even by an Englishman of Englishmen. It was
thoroughly justified by the event, and, I may perhaps
be permitted to observe, ran exactly contrary to a
sentiment rather widely adopted of late. No man,
whether in public writings or private conduct, could
be more set than Scott was against a spurious Scotch
particularism. He even earned from silly Scots
maledictions for the chivalrous justice he dealt to
England in *The Lord of the Isles*, and the common-

sense justice he dealt to her in the mouth of Bailie Jarvie. But he was not more staunch for the political Union than he was for the preservation of minor institutions, manners, and character; and the proposed interference with Scotch banking seemed to him to be one of the things tending to make good Scotchmen, as he bluntly told Croker, 'damned mischievous Englishmen.' Therefore he arose and spoke, and though he averted the immediate attempt, yet the prophecies which he uttered were amply fulfilled in other ways after the Reform Bill.

These, then, are the principles on which I have selected the pieces that follow (some minor reasons for the particular choices being given in the special introductions):—That they should be pamphlets proper (*Malachi* appeared first in a newspaper, but that was a sign of the time chiefly, and the numbers of Cobbett's *Register* were practically independent pieces); that they should deal with special subjects of burning political, and not merely personal, interest; and that they should either directly or in the long-run have exercised an actual determining influence on the course of politics and history. This last point is undoubted in the case of the examples from Halifax, Swift, Burke (who more than any one man pointed and steeled the

resistance of England to Jacobin tyranny), and Scott ;
it was less immediate, but scarcely more dubious in
those of Defoe, Cobbett, and Sydney Smith.   And
so in all humility I make my bow as introducer once
more to the English public of these Seven Masters
of English political writing.

I.—'LETTER TO A DISSENTER'

By George Savile, Marquess of Halifax

(There is no doubt that Halifax's work deserves to rank first in a collection of political pamphlets. He signed none; it was indeed almost impossible for a prominent person in the State then safely or decently to do so, and different attributions were made at the time of some of them, as of the Character of a Trimmer *to Coventry, and of this* Letter *(this 'masterly little tract,' as Macaulay justly calls it) to Temple. But shortly after his death all were published as his unchallenged, and there never has been any doubt of their authorship in the minds of good judges. Four of them are so good that extrinsic reasons have to be brought in for preferring one to the other. The* Character of a Trimmer *is rather too long for my scheme; the* Anatomy *of an* Equivalent *is too technical, and requires too much illustration and exegesis; the* Cautions for Choice of Members of Parliament, *though practically valuable to*

the present day, is a little too general.   The Letter to
a Dissenter *escapes all these objections.   It is brief, it
is thoroughly to the point, it is comprehensible almost
without note or comment to any one who remembers the
broad fact that by his Declaration of Indulgence James
the Second attempted to detach, and almost succeeded in
detaching, the Dissenters from their common cause
with the Church in opposing his enfranchisement of the
Roman Catholics, and his preferment of them to great
offices.   As for its author, his most eminent acts are
written in the pages of the universally read historian
above quoted.   But he was in reality more of a Tory
than it suited Macaulay to represent him, though he
gloried in the name of Trimmer, and certainly showed
what is called in modern political slang a 'crossbench mind'
not only during the madness of the Popish plot, during
the greater madness of James's assaults on the Church,
the Constitution, and private rights, but also (after the
Revolution) towards William of Orange.   Born about
1630 he died in April 1695, leaving the fame, unjusti-
fied by any samples in those unreported days, of the
greatest orator of his time, a reputation as a wit which
was partly inherited by his grandson, Chesterfield, and
the small volume of* Miscellanies, *on which we here
draw.   The pamphlet itself appeared in April* 1687.)

A LETTER TO A DISSENTER, UPON OCCASION
OF HIS MAJESTY'S LATE GRACIOUS DECLARA-
TION OF INDULGENCE

SIR—Since addresses are in fashion, give me leave
to make one to you. This is neither the effect of fear,
interest, or resentment; therefore you may be sure it
is sincere: and for that reason it may expect to be
kindly received. Whether it will have power enough
to convince, dependeth upon the reasons of which
you are to judge; and upon your preparation of mind,
to be persuaded by truth, whenever it appeareth to
you. It ought not to be the less welcome for coming
from a friendly hand, one whose kindness to you is
not lessened by difference of opinion, and who will
not let his thoughts for the public be so tied or confined to this or that sub-division of Protestants as to
stifle the charity, which besides all other arguments,
is at this time become necessary to preserve us.

I am neither surprised nor provoked, to see that
in the condition you were put into by the laws, and
the ill circumstances you lay under, by having the
Exclusion and Rebellion laid to your charge, you were
desirous to make yourselves less uneasy and obnoxious to authority. Men who are sore, run to the
nearest remedy with too much haste to consider all
the consequences: grains of allowance are to be

given, where nature giveth such strong influences. When to men under sufferings it offereth ease, the present pain will hardly allow time to examine the remedies; and the strongest reason can hardly gain a fair audience from our mind, whilst so possessed, till the smart is a little allayed.

I do not know whether the warmth that naturally belongeth to new friendships, may not make it a harder task for me to persuade you. It is like telling lovers, in the beginning of their joys, that they will in a little time have an end. Such an unwelcome style doth not easily find credit. But I will suppose you are not so far gone in your new passion, but that you will hear still; and therefore I am also under the less discouragement, when I offer to your consideration two things. The *first* is, the cause you have to suspect your new friends. The *second*, the duty incumbent upon you, in Christianity and prudence, not to hazard the public safety, neither by desire of ease nor of revenge.

To the *first*. Consider that notwithstanding the smooth language which is now put on to engage you, these new friends did not make you their choice, but their refuge. They have ever made their first courtships to the Church of England, and when they were rejected there, they made their application to you in the second place. The instances of this might be given in all times. I do not repeat them, because whatsoever is unnecessary must be tedious ; the truth of this assertion being so plain as not to admit a dispute. You cannot therefore reasonably flatter yourselves that there is any inclination to you. They never pretended to allow you any quarter, but to usher in liberty for themselves under that shelter. I refer you to Mr. Coleman's Letters, and to the Journals of Parliament, where you may be convinced, if you can be so mistaken as to doubt ; nay, at this very hour they can hardly forbear, in the height of their courtship, to let fall hard words of you. So little is nature to be restrained ; it will start out sometimes, disdaining to submit to the usurpation of art and interest.

This alliance, between liberty and infallibility, is bringing together the two most contrary things that are in the world. The Church of Rome doth not only dislike the allowing liberty, but by its prin-ciples it cannot do it. Wine is not more expressly forbid to the Mahometans, than giving heretics liberty to the Papists. They are no more able to make good their vows to you, than men married before, and their wife alive, can confirm their contract with another. The continuance of their kindness would be a habit of sin, of which they are to repent ; and their absolution is to be had upon no other terms than their promise to destroy you. You are therefore to be hugged now, only that you may be the better squeezed at another time. There must be something extraordinary when the Church of Rome setteth up bills, and offereth plaisters, for tender consciences. By all that hath hitherto appeared, her skill in chirurgery lieth chiefly in a quick hand to cut off limbs; but she is the worst at healing of any that ever pretended to it.

To come so quick from another extreme is such an unnatural motion that you ought to be upon your guard. The other day you were Sons of Belial; now you are Angels of Light. This is a violent change, and it will be fit for you to pause upon it before you believe it. If your features are not altered, neither is their opinion of you, whatever may be pretended. Do you believe less than you did that there is idolatry in the Church of Rome? Sure you do not. See, then, how they treat, both in words and writing, those who entertain that opinion. Conclude from hence, how inconsistent their favour is with this single article, except they give you a dispensation for this too, and not by a *non obstante*, secure you that they will not think the worse of you.

Think a little how dangerous it is to build upon a foundation of paradoxes. Popery now is the only friend to liberty, and the known enemy to persecution. The men of Taunton and Tiverton are above all other eminent for Loyalty. The Quakers, from being declared by the Papists not to be Christians,

are now made favourites, and taken into their particular protection; they are on a sudden grown the
most accomplished men of the kingdom in good
breeding, and give thanks with the best grace in
double-refined language. So that I should not
wonder, though a man of that persuasion, in spite of
his hat, should be Master of the Ceremonies. Not
to say harsher words, these are such very new things,
that it is impossible not to suspend our belief, till by
a little more experience, we may be informed whether
they are realities or apparitions. We have been
under shameful mistakes, if these opinions are true;
but for the present we are apt to be incredulous,
except that we could be convinced that the priest's
words in this case too are able to make such a
sudden and effectual change; and that their power is
not limited to the Sacrament, but that it extendeth to
alter the nature of all other things, as often as they
are so disposed.

Let me now speak of the instruments of your
friendship, and then leave you to judge whether they
do not afford matter of suspicion. No sharpness is
to be mingled, where healing only is intended; so
nothing will be said to expose particular men, how
strong soever the temptation may be, or how clear
the proofs to make it out. A word or two in general,
for your better caution, shall suffice. Suppose then,
for argument's sake, that the mediators of this new

alliance should be such as have been formerly employed in treaties of the same kind, and there detected to have acted by order, and to have been empowered to give encouragements and rewards. Would not this be an argument to suspect them?

If they should plainly be under engagements to one side, their arguments to the other ought to be received accordingly. Their fair pretences are to be looked upon as a part of their commission, which may not improbably give them a dispensation in the case of truth, when it may bring a prejudice upon the service of those by whom they are employed.

If there should be men, who having formerly had means and authority to persuade by secular arguments, have, in pursuance of that power, sprinkled money among the Dissenting ministers; and if those very men should now have the same authority, practise the same methods, and disburse where they cannot otherwise persuade; it seemeth to me to be rather an evidence than a presumption of the deceit.

If there should be ministers amongst you, who by having fallen under temptations of this kind, are in some sort engaged to continue their frailty, by the awe they are in lest it should be exposed; the persuasions of these unfortunate men must sure have the less force, and their arguments, though never so specious, are to be suspected, when they come from men who have mortgaged themselves to severe creditors, that expect a rigorous observance of the contract, let it be never so unwarrantable. If these, or any others, should at this time preach up anger and vengeance against the Church of England; may it not without injustice be suspected that a thing so plainly out of season springeth rather from corruption than mistake; and that those who act this choleric part, do not believe themselves, but only pursue higher directions, and endeavour to make good that part of their contract, which obligeth them, upon a forfeiture, to make use of their enflaming eloquence? They might apprehend their wages would be retrenched if they should be moderate: and therefore, whilst violence is their interest, those who have not the same arguments have no reason to follow such a partial example.

If there should be men, who by the load of their crimes against the Government, have been bowed down to comply with it against their conscience; who by incurring the want of a pardon, have drawn upon themselves a necessity of an entire resignation, such men are to be lamented, but not to be believed. Nay, they themselves, when they have discharged their unwelcome talk, will be inwardly glad that their forced endeavours do not succeed, and are pleased when men resist their insinuations; which are far from being voluntary or sincere, but are squeezed out of them by the weight of their being so obnoxious.

If, in the height of this great dearness, by comparing things, it should happen that at this instant there is much a surer friendship with those who are so far from allowing liberty that they allow no living to a Protestant under them—let the scene lie in what part of the world it will, the argument will come home, and sure it will afford sufficient ground to suspect.   Apparent contradictions must strike us ; neither nature nor reason can digest them.   Self-flattery, and the desire to deceive ourselves, to gratify present appetite, with all their power, which is great, cannot get the better of such broad conviction, as some things carry along with them.   Will you call these vain and empty suspicions?   Have you been at all times so void of fears and jealousies, as to justify your being so unreasonably valiant in having none upon this occasion?   Such an extraordinary courage at this unseasonable time, to say no more, is too dangerous a virtue to be commended.

If then, for these and a thousand other reasons, there is cause to suspect, sure your new friends are not to dictate to you, or advise you.   For instance : the Addresses that fly abroad every week, and murder us with *another to the same* ; the first draughts are made by those who are not very proper to be secretaries to the Protestant Religion : and it is your part only to write them out fairer again.

Strange ! that you, who have been formerly so

much against *set forms*, should now be content the
priests should indite for you. The nature of thanks
is an unavoidable consequence of being pleased or
obliged; they grow in the heart, and from thence
show themselves either in looks, speech, writing, or
action. No man was ever thankful because he was
bid to be so, but because he had, or thought he had
some reason for it. If then there is cause in this
case to pay such extravagant acknowledgments, they
will flow naturally, without taking such pains to procure them; and it is unkindly done to tire all the
Post-horses with carrying circular letters, to solicit that
which would be done without any trouble or con-
straint. If it is really in itself such a favour, what
needeth so much pressing men to be thankful, and
with such eager circumstances, that where persuasions
cannot delude, threatenings are employed to fright
them into a compliance? Thanks must be voluntary,
not only unconstrained but unsolicited, else they are
either trifles or snares, that either signify nothing or
a great deal more than is intended by those that give
them. If an inference should be made, that whoso-
ever thanketh the King for his Declaration, is by that
engaged to justify it in point of law; it is a greater
stride than I presume all those care to make who are
persuaded to address. It shall be supposed that all
the thankers will be repealers of the Test, whenever
a Parliament shall meet; such an expectation is better

prevented before than disappointed afterwards; and
the surest way to avoid the lying under such a
scandal is not to do anything that may give a
colour to the mistake.   These bespoken thanks are
little less improper than love-letters that were solicited
by the lady to whom they are to be directed: so
that, besides the little ground there is to give them,
the manner of getting them doth extremely lessen
their value.   It might be wished that you would have
suppressed your impatience, and have been content,
for the sake of religion, to enjoy it within yourselves,
without the liberty of a public exercise, till a Parliament had allowed it; but since that could not be,
and that the articles of some amongst you have made
use of the well-meant zeal of the generality to draw
them into this mistake, I am so far from blaming
you with that sharpness, which perhaps the matter in
strictness would bear, that I am ready to err on the
side of the more gentle construction.

There is a great difference between enjoying quietly
the advantages of an act irregularly done by others,
and the going about to support it against the laws in
being.   The law is so sacred that no trespass against
it is to be defended; yet frailties may in some measure
be excused when they cannot be justified.   The
desire of enjoying liberty, from which men have been
so long restrained, may be a temptation that their
reason is not at all times able to resist.   If in such a

case some objections are leapt over, indifferent men will be more inclined to lament the occasion than to fall too hard upon the fault, whilst it is covered with the apology of a good intention. But where, to rescue yourselves from the severity of one law, you give a blow to all the laws, by which your religion and liberty are to be protected; and instead of silently receiving the benefit of this indulgence, you set up for advocates to support it, you become voluntary aggressors, and look like counsel retained by the prerogative against your old friend Magna Charta, who hath done nothing to deserve her falling thus under your displeasure.

If the case then should be, that the price expected from you for this liberty is giving up your right in the laws, sure you will think twice before you go any further in such a losing bargain. After giving thanks for the breach of one law, you lose the right of complaining of the breach of all the rest; you will not very well know how to defend yourselves when you are pressed; and having given up the question when it was for your advantage, you cannot recall it when it shall be to your prejudice. If you will set up at one time a power to help you, which at another time, by parity of reason, shall be made use of to destroy you, you will neither be pitied nor relieved against a mischief which you draw upon yourselves by being so unreasonably thankful. It is like calling in auxiliaries to help, who are strong enough to subdue you. In such a case your complaints will come too late to be heard, and your sufferings will raise mirth instead of compassion.

If you think, for your excuse, to expound your thanks, so as to restrain them to this particular case; others, for their ends, will extend them further : and in these differing interpretations, that which is backed by authority will be the most likely to prevail ; especially when, by the advantage you have given them, they have in truth the better of the argument, and that the inferences from your own concessions are very strong and express against you. This is so far from being a groundless supposition, that there was a late instance of it in the last session of Parliament, in the House of Lords, where the first thanks, though things of course, were interpreted to be the approbation of the King's whole speech, and a restraint from the further examination of any part of it, though never so much disliked ; and it was with difficulty obtained, not to be excluded from the liberty of objecting to this mighty prerogative of dispensing, merely by this innocent and usual piece of good manners, by which no such thing could possibly be intended.

This showeth that some bounds are to be put to your good breeding, and that the Constitution of England is too valuable a thing to be ventured upon a compliment. Now that you have for some time enjoyed the benefit of the end, it is time for you to look into the danger of the means. The same reason that made you desirous to get liberty must make you solicitous to preserve it, so that the next thought will naturally be, not to engage yourself beyond retreat ; and to agree so far with the principles of all religion, as not to rely upon a death-bed repentance.

There are certain periods of time, which being once past, make all cautions ineffectual, and all remedies desperate. Our understandings are apt to be hurried on by the first heats, which, if not restrained in time, do not give us leave to look back till it is too late. Consider this in the case of your anger against the Church of England, and take warning by their mistake in the same kind, when after the late King's Restoration they preserved so long the bitter taste of your rough usage to them in other times, that it made them forget their interest and sacrifice it to their revenge.

Either you will blame this proceeding in them, and for that reason not follow it ; or, if you allow it, you have no reason to be offended with them ; so that you must either dismiss your anger or lose your excuse ; except you should argue more partially than will be supposed of men of your morality and under-standing.

If you had now to do with those rigid prelates who made it a matter of conscience to give you the

least indulgence, but kept you at an uncharitable
distance, and even to your most reasonable scruples
continued stiff and inexorable, the argument might be
fairer on your side; but since the common danger
has so laid open that mistake, that all the former
haughtiness towards you is for ever extinguished, and
that it hath turned the spirit of persecution into a
spirit of peace, charity, and condescension; shall
this happy change only affect the Church of England?
And are you so in love with separation as not to be
moved by this example? It ought to be followed,
were there no other reason than that it is virtue; but
when, besides that, it is become necessary to your
preservation, it is impossible to fail the having its
effect upon you.

If it should be said that the Church of England
is never humble but when she is out of power, and
therefore loseth the right of being believed when she
pretendeth to it: the answer is, *first*, It would be an
uncharitable objection, and very much mistimed; an
unseasonable triumph, not only ungenerous but un-
safe: so that in these respects it cannot be urged
without scandal, even though it could be said with
truth. *Secondly*, This is not so in fact, and the argument must fall, being built upon a false foundation;
for whatever may be told you at this very hour, and
in the heat and glare of your perfect sunshine, the
Church of England can in a moment bring clouds

again, and turn the royal thunder upon your heads,
blow you off the stage with a breath, if she would
give but a smile or a kind word; the least glimpse of
her compliance would throw you back into the state
of suffering, and draw upon you all the arrears of
severity which have accrued during the time of this
kindness to you; and yet the Church of England,
with all her faults, will not allow herself to be rescued
by such unjustifiable means, but chooseth to bear the
weight of power rather than lie under the burden of
being criminal.

It cannot be said that she is unprovoked: books
and letters come out every day to call for answers,
yet she will not be stirred. From the supposed
authors and the style, one would swear they were
undertakers, and had made a contract to fall out with
the Church of England. There are lashes in every
address, challenges to draw the pen in every pamphlet. In short, the fairest occasions in the world
given to quarrel; but she wisely distinguisheth between
the body of Dissenters, whom she will suppose to act,
as they do, with no ill intent, and these small skir-
mishers, picked and sent out to piqueer, and to
begin a fray amongst the Protestants for the enter-
tainment as well as the advantage of the Church
of Rome.

This conduct is so good, that it will be scandalous
not to applaud it. It is not equal dealing to blame

C

our adversaries for doing ill, and not commend them when they do well.

To hate them because they are persecuted, and not to be reconciled to them when they are ready to suffer rather than receive all the advantages that can be gained by a criminal compliance, is a principle no sort of Christians can own, since it would give an objection to them never to be answered.

Think a little who they were that promoted your former persecutions, and then consider how it will look to be angry with the instruments, and at the same time to make a league with the authors of your sufferings.

Have you enough considered what will be expected from you ?   Are you ready to stand in every borough by virtue of a *congé d'élire*, and instead of election be satisfied if you are returned ?

Will you, in parliament, justify the dispensing power, with all its consequences, and repeal the test, by which you will make way for the repeal of all the laws that were made to preserve your religion, and to enact others that shall destroy it ?

Are you disposed to change the liberty of debate into the merit of obedience ; and to be made instruments to repeal or enact laws, when the Roman Consistory are Lords of the Articles ?

Are you so linked to your new friends as to reject any indulgence a parliament shall offer you, if it shall not be so comprehensive as to include the Papists in it?

Consider that the implied conditions of your new treaty are no less than that you are to do everything you are desired, without examining; and that for this pretended liberty of conscience, your real freedom is to be sacrificed; your former faults hang like chains still about you, you are let loose only upon bail; the first act of non-compliance sendeth you to gaol again.

You may see that the Papists themselves do not rely upon the legality of this power which you are to justify, since the being so very earnest to get it established by a law, and the doing such very hard things in order, as they think, to obtain it, is a clear evidence that they do not think that the single power of the Crown is in this case a good foundation; especially when this is done under a prince so very tender of the rights of sovereignty that he would think it a diminution to his prerogative, where he conceiveth it strong enough to go alone, to call in the legislative help to strengthen and support it.

You have formerly blamed the Church of England, and not without reason, for going so far as they did in their compliance; and yet so soon as they stopped, you see they are not only deserted, but prosecuted. Conclude, then, from this example, that you must either break off your friendship or resolve to have no

bounds in it.   If they do succeed in their design,
they will leave you first : if they do, you must either
leave them, when it will be too late for your safety,
or else, after the squeaziness of starting at a surplice,
you must be forced to swallow Transubstantiation.

Remember that the other day those of the Church
of England were Trimmers for enduring you; and
now, by a sudden turn, you are become the favourites.
Do not deceive yourselves; it is not the nature of
lasting plants thus to shoot up in a night; you may
look gay and green for a little time, but you want a
root to give you a continuance.   It is not so long
since, as to be forgotten, that the maxim was, It is
impossible for a Dissenter not to be a REBEL.   Consider at this time in France, even the new converts
are so far from being employed that they are disarmed ; their sudden change maketh them still to be
distrusted, notwithstanding that they are reconciled ;
what are you to expect then from your dear friends,
to whom, whenever they shall think fit to throw you
off again, you have in other times given such arguments for their excuse ?

Besides all this you act very unskilfully against
your visible interest, if you throw away the advantages
of which you can hardly fail in the next probable
Revolution.   Things tend naturally to what you
would have, if you would let them alone, and not by
an unseasonable activity lose the influences of your

good star, which promiseth you everything that is prosperous.

The Church of England, convinced of its error in being severe to you; the Parliament, whenever it meeteth sure to be gentle to you; the next heir, bred in the country which you have so often quoted for a pattern of indulgence; a general agreement of all thinking men, that we must no more cut ourselves off from the Protestants abroad, but rather enlarge the foundations upon which we are to build our defences against the common enemy; so that in truth, all things seem to conspire to give you ease and satisfaction, if by too much haste to anticipate your good fortune you do not destroy it.

The Protestants have but one article of human strength to oppose the power which is now against them, and that is not to lose the advantage of their numbers by being so unwary as to let themselves be divided.

We all agree in our duty to our prince; our objections to his belief do not hinder us from seeing his virtues; and our not complying with his religion hath no effect upon our allegiance. We are not to be laughed out of our passive obedience, and the doctrine of non-resistance, though even those who perhaps owe the best part of their security to that principle are apt to make a jest of it.

So that if we give no advantage by the fatal

mistake of misapplying our anger, by the natural course of things; this danger will pass away like a shower of hail; fair weather will succeed, as lowering as the sky now looketh, and all this by a plain and easy receipt. Let us be still, quiet, and undivided, firm at the same time to our religion, our loyalty, and our laws; and so long as we continue this method it is next to impossible that the odds of two hundred to one should lose the bet; except the Church of Rome, which hath been so long barren of miracles, should now, in her declining age, be brought to bed of one that would outdo the best she can brag of in her legend.

To conclude, the short question will be, Whether you will join with those who must in the end run the same fate with you? If Protestants of all sorts, in their behaviour to one another, have been to blame, they are upon more equal terms, and, for that very reason, it is fitter for them now to be reconciled. Our disunion is not only a reproach, but a danger to us. Those who believe in modern miracles have more right, or at least more excuse, to neglect all secular caution; but for us, it is as justifiable to have no religion as wilfully to throw away the human means of preserving it.—I am, Dear Sir, your most affectionate humble Servant,   T. W.

II.—'THE SHORTEST WAY WITH THE DISSENTERS'

By Daniel Defoe

(Defoe wrote an enormous number of pamphlets; for great part of his life he might almost have been described as a pamphleteer pure and simple. In the vast lists of publications which his biographers and bibliographers have compiled, partly by industry and partly by imagination, by far the larger number of entries is of the pamphlet kind. Indeed, as most people know, Defoe did not take to the composition of the fiction which has made his name famous till very late in life. Born in the year 1661, *he began pamphleteering when he was scarcely of age, and continued in that way (with occasional excursions into work larger in scale, but not very different in style or matter) for nearly forty years before the publication of* Robinson Crusoe. *His two most famous and most effective pamphlets were the so-called* Legion Letter *and* The Shortest Way with the Dissenters *(given here), to which may perhaps be added the* Reasons against War with France. *All these, with many others, appeared within the compass*

of the years 1700-1702. *The three together touched
upon the three most burning questions of the late seventeenth and early eighteenth centuries—parliamentary
factiousness, an aggressive policy abroad, and toleration
at home.   Little or no annotation is required for their
comprehension, but the reader may amuse himself if he
likes by meditating whether the* Shortest Way *is irony
or not.   My own opinion is that it is not ; being a
simple statement of the actual views of the other side.
The anecdotic history of the piece—how it was taken for
serious by both sides, was prosecuted by Government,
the author proclaimed, and a reward offered for his
detection ; how, the printer and publisher being arrested,
Defoe surrendered, was tried, pleaded guilty, was fined,
pilloried, and imprisoned—may be read in the biogra-
phies.   His imprisonment lasted till August* 1704, *when
Harley let him out, and he entered upon a course of
rather mysterious service as a Government free-lance,
which was continued under various ministries, and has
not on the whole brought him credit with posterity.
For many years, his remarkable* Review, *a political
journal which he conducted single-handed, served as his
chief organ ; but he never gave up writing pamphlets
till his death in* 1731, *though he never approached either
the merit or the effect of that here given.*)

Sir Roger L'Estrange tells us a story in his collection of fables, of the cock and the horses.   The cock

was gotten to roost in the stable among the horses, and there being no racks or other conveniences for him, it seems he was forced to roost upon the ground. The horses jostling about for room, and putting the cock in danger of his life, he gives them this grave advice, 'Pray, gentlefolks, let us stand still, for fear we should tread upon one another.'

There are some people in the world, who now they are unperched, and reduced to an equality with other people, and under strong and very just apprehensions of being further treated as they deserve, begin, with Æsop's cock, to preach up peace and union, and the Christian duties of moderation, forgetting that, when they had the power in their hands, these graces were strangers in their gates.

It is now near fourteen years that the glory and peace of the purest and most flourishing Church in the world has been eclipsed, buffeted, and disturbed by a sort of men whom God in His providence has suffered to insult over her and bring her down. These have been the days of her humiliation and tribulation. She has borne with invincible patience the reproach of the wicked, and God has at last heard her prayers, and delivered her from the oppression of the stranger.

And now they find their day is over, their power gone, and the throne of this nation possessed by a royal, English, true, and ever-constant member of, and

friend to, the Church of England. Now they find that
they are in danger of the Church of England's just
resentments; now they cry out peace, union, forbear-
ance, and charity, as if the Church had not too long
harboured her enemies under her wing, and nourished
the viperous brood till they hiss and fly in the face of
the mother that cherished them.

No, gentlemen, the time of mercy is past, your
day of grace is over; you should have practised
peace, and moderation, and charity, if you expected
any yourselves.

We have heard none of this lesson for fourteen
years past. We have been huffed and bullied with
your Act of Toleration; you have told us that you
are the Church established by law, as well as others;
have set up your canting synagogues at our church
doors, and the Church and members have been loaded
with reproaches, with oaths, associations, abjurations,
and what not. Where has been the mercy, the for-
bearance, the charity, you have shown to tender consciences of the Church of England, that could not
take oaths as fast as you made them; that having
sworn allegiance to their lawful and rightful King,
could not dispense with that oath, their King being
still alive, and swear to your new hodge-podge of a
Dutch Government? These have been turned out
of their livings, and they and their families left to
starve; their estates double taxed to carry on a war

they had no hand in, and you got nothing by. What account can you give of the multitudes you have forced to comply, against their consciences, with your new sophistical politics, who, like new converts in France, sin because they cannot starve? And now the tables are turned upon you; you must not be persecuted; it is not a Christian spirit.

You have butchered one king, deposed another king, and made a mock king of a third, and yet you could have the face to expect to be employed and trusted by the fourth. Anybody that did not know the temper of your party would stand amazed at the impudence, as well as folly, to think of it.

Your management of your Dutch monarch, whom you reduced to a mere King of Clouts, is enough to give any future princes such an idea of your principles as to warn them sufficiently from coming into your clutches; and God be thanked the Queen is out of your hands, knows you, and will have a care of you.

There is no doubt but the supreme authority of a nation has in itself a power, and a right to that power, to execute the laws upon any part of that nation it governs. The execution of the known laws of the land, and that with a weak and gentle hand neither, was all this fanatical party of this land have ever called persecution; this they have magnified to a height, that the sufferings of the Huguenots in France were not to be compared with. Now, to execute the known laws of a nation upon those who transgress them, after voluntarily consenting to the making those laws, can never be called persecution, but justice. But justice is always violence to the party offending, for every man is innocent in his own eyes. The first execution of the laws against Dissenters in England was in the days of King James the First; and what did it amount to truly? The worst they suffered was at their own request : to let them go to New England and erect a new colony, and give them great privileges, grants, and suitable powers, keep them under protection, and defend them against all invaders, and receive no taxes or revenue from them. This was the cruelty of the Church of England. Fatal leniency! It was the ruin of that excellent prince, King Charles the First. Had King James sent all the Puritans in England away to the West Indies, we had been a national, unmixed Church; the Church of England had been kept undivided and entire.

To requite the lenity of the father they take up arms against the son ; conquer, pursue, take, imprison, and at last put to death the anointed of God, and destroy the very being and nature of government, setting up a sordid impostor, who had neither title to govern nor understanding to manage, but supplied that want with power, bloody and desperate counsels, and craft without conscience.

Had not King James the First withheld the full execution of the laws, had he given them strict justice, he had cleared the nation of them, and the consequences had been plain : his son had never been murdered by them nor the monarchy overwhelmed. It was too much mercy shown them was the ruin of his posterity and the ruin of the nation's peace. One would think the Dissenters should not have the face to believe that we are to be wheedled and canted into peace and toleration when they know that they have once requited us with a civil war, and once with an intolerable and unrighteous persecution for our former civility.

Nay, to encourage us to be easy with them, it is apparent that they never had the upper hand of the Church, but they treated her with all the severity, with all the reproach and contempt that was possible. What peace and what mercy did they show the loyal gentry of the Church of England in the time of their triumphant Commonwealth? How did they put all the gentry of England to ransom, whether they were actually in arms for the King or not, making people compound for their estates and starve their families? How did they treat the clergy of the Church of England, sequestered the ministers, devoured the patrimony of the Church, and divided the spoil by sharing the Church lands among their soldiers, and turning her clergy out to starve? Just such measure as they have meted should be measured them again.

Charity and love is the known doctrine of the Church of England, and it is plain she has put it in practice towards the Dissenters, even beyond what they ought, till she has been wanting to herself, and in effect unkind to her sons, particularly in the too much lenity of King James the First, mentioned before. Had he so rooted the Puritans from the face of the land, which he had an opportunity early to have done, they had not had the power to vex the Church as since they have done.

In the days of King Charles the Second how did the Church reward their bloody doings with lenity and mercy, except the barbarous regicides of the pretended court of justice? Not a soul suffered for all the blood in an unnatural war. King Charles came in all mercy and love, cherished them, preferred them, employed them, withheld the rigour of the law, and oftentimes, even against the advice of his Parliament, gave them liberty of conscience; and how did they requite him with the villanous contrivance to depose and murder him and his successor at the Rye Plot?

King James, as if mercy was the inherent quality of the family, began his reign with unusual favour to them. Nor could their joining with the Duke of Monmouth against him move him to do himself justice upon them; but that mistaken prince thought to win them by gentleness and love, proclaimed an universal liberty to them, and rather discountenanced the Church of England than them. How they requited him all the world knows.

The late reign is too fresh in the memory of all the world to need a comment; how, under pretence of joining with the Church in redressing some griev- ances, they pushed things to that extremity, in con- junction with some mistaken gentlemen, as to depose the late King, as if the grievance of the nation could not have been redressed but by the absolute ruin of the prince. Here is an instance of their temper, their peace, and charity. To what height they carried themselves during the reign of a king of their own; how they crept into all places of trust and profit; how they insinuated into the favour of the King, and were at first preferred to the highest places in the nation; how they engrossed the ministry, and above all, how pitifully they managed, is too plain to need any remarks.

But particularly their mercy and charity, the spirit of union, they tell us so much of, has been remarkable in Scotland. If any man would see the spirit of a Dissenter, let him look into Scotland. There they made entire conquest of the Church, trampled down the sacred orders, and suppressed the Episcopal government with an absolute, and, as they suppose, irretrievable victory, though it is possible they may find themselves mistaken. Now it would be a very proper question to ask their impudent advocate, the

Observator, pray how much mercy and favour did the members of the Episcopal Church find in Scotland from the Scotch Presbyterian Government? and I shall undertake for the Church of England that the Dissenters shall still receive as much here, though they deserve but little.

In a small treatise of the sufferings of the Episcopal clergy in Scotland, it will appear what usage they met with; how they not only lost their livings, but in several places were plundered and abused in their persons; the ministers that could not conform turned out with numerous families and no maintenance, and hardly charity enough left to relieve them with a bit of bread. And the cruelties of the parties are innumerable, and not to be attempted in this short piece.

And now to prevent the distant cloud which they perceived to hang over their heads from England, with a true Presbyterian policy they put in for a union of nations, that England might unite their Church with the Kirk of Scotland, and their Presbyterian members sit in our House of Commons, and their Assembly of Scotch canting long-cloaks in our Convocation. What might have been if our fanatic Whiggish statesmen continued, God only knows; but we hope we are out of fear of that now.

It is alleged by some of the faction—and they began to bully us with it—that if we won't unite with them they will not settle the crown with us again, but when Her Majesty dies, will choose a king for themselves.

If they won't, we must make them, and it is not the first time we have let them know that we are able. The crowns of these kingdoms have not so far disowned the right of succession but they may retrieve it again ; and if Scotland thinks to come off from a successive to an elective state of government, England has not promised not to assist the right heir and put them into possession without any regard to their ridiculous settlements.

These are the gentlemen, these their ways of treating the Church, both at home and abroad. Now let us examine the reasons they pretend to give why we should be favourable to them, why we should continue and tolerate them among us.

First, they are very numerous, they say ; they are a great part of the nation, and we cannot suppress them.

To this may be answered :—

1. They are not so numerous as the Protestants in France, and yet the French King effectually cleared the nation of them at once, and we don't find he misses them at home. But I am not of the opinion they are so numerous as is pretended ; their party is more numerous than their persons, and those mistaken people of the Church who are misled and deluded by

D

their wheedling artifices to join with them, make their party the greater ; but these will open their eyes when the Government shall set heartily about the work, and come off from them, as some animals, which they say always desert a house when it is likely to fall.

2. The more numerous the more dangerous, and therefore the more need to suppress them ; and God has suffered us to bear them as goads in our sides for not utterly extinguishing them long ago.

3. If we are to allow them only because we cannot suppress them, then it ought to be tried whether we can or not ; and I am of opinion it is easy to be done, and could prescribe ways and means, if it were proper ; but I doubt not the Government will find effectual methods for the rooting the contagion from the face of this land.

Another argument they use, which is this, that it is a time of war, and we have need to unite against the common enemy.

We answer, this common enemy had been no enemy if they had not made him so. He was quiet, in peace, and no way disturbed or encroached upon us, and we know no reason we had to quarrel with him.

But further, we make no question but we are able to deal with this common enemy without their help ; but why must we unite with them because of the enemy? Will they go over to the enemy if we do not prevent it by a union with them? We are very well contented they should, and make no question we shall be ready to deal with them and the common enemy too, and better without them than with them.

Besides, if we have a common enemy, there is the more need to be secure against our private enemies. If there is one common enemy, we have the less need to have an enemy in our bowels.

It was a great argument some people used against suppressing the old money, that it was a time of war, and it was too great a risk for the nation to run; if we should not master it, we should be undone. And yet the sequel proved the hazard was not so great but it might be mastered, and the success was answerable. The suppressing the Dissenters is not a harder work nor a work of less necessity to the public. We can never enjoy a settled, uninterrupted union and tranquillity in this nation till the spirit of Whiggism, faction, and schism is melted down like the old money.

To talk of the difficulty is to frighten ourselves with chimeras and notions of a powerful party, which are indeed a party without power. Difficulties often appear greater at a distance than when they are searched into with judgment and distinguished from the vapours and shadows that attend them.

We are not to be frightened with it; this age is wiser than that by all our own experience and theirs

too.   King Charles the First had early suppressed
this party if he had taken more deliberate measures.
In short, it is not worth arguing to talk of their arms.
Their Monmouths, and Shaftesburys, and Argyles are
gone; their Dutch sanctuary is at an end; Heaven
has made way for their destruction, and if we do not
close with the Divine occasion we are to blame ourselves, and may remember that we had once an
opportunity to serve the Church of England by
extirpating her implacable enemies, and having let
slip the minute that Heaven presented, may experi-
mentally complain, *Post est occasio calva.*

Here are some popular objections in the way :—

As first, the Queen has promised them to continue
them in their tolerated liberty, and has told us she
will be a religious observer of her word.

What Her Majesty will do we cannot help; but
what, as head of the Church, she ought to do, is
another case.   Her Majesty has promised to protect
and defend the Church of England, and if she cannot
effectually do that without the destruction of the Dissenters, she must of course dispense with one promise
to comply with another.   But to answer this cavil
more effectually : Her Majesty did never promise to
maintain the toleration to the destruction of the
Church ; but it is upon supposition that it may be
compatible with the well-being and safety of the
Church, which she had declared she would take

especial care of. Now if these two interests clash, it is plain Her Majesty's intentions are to uphold, protect, defend, and establish the Church, and this we conceive is impossible.

Perhaps it may be said that the Church is in no immediate danger from the Dissenters, and therefore it is time enough. But this is a weak answer.

For first, if a danger be real, the distance of it is no argument against, but rather a spur to quicken us to prevention, lest it be too late hereafter.

And secondly, here is the opportunity, and the only one perhaps that ever the Church had, to secure herself and destroy her enemies.

The representatives of the nation have now an opportunity; the time is come which all good men have wished for, that the gentlemen of England may serve the Church of England. Now they are protected and encouraged by a Church of England Queen.

What will you do for your sister in the day that she shall be spoken for?

If ever you will establish the best Christian Church in the world; if ever you will suppress the spirit of enthusiasm; if ever you will free the nation from the viperous brood that have so long sucked the blood of their mother; if ever you will leave your posterity free from faction and rebellion, this is the time. This is the time to pull up this heretical weed of sedition that has so long disturbed the peace of our Church and poisoned the good corn.

But, says another hot and cold objector, this is renewing fire and faggot, reviving the act *De Heretico Comburendo*; this will be cruelty in its nature, and barbarous to all the world.

I answer, it is cruelty to kill a snake or a toad in cold blood, but the poison of their nature makes it a charity to our neighbours to destroy those creatures, not for any personal injury received, but for prevention; not for the evil they have done, but the evil they may do.

Serpents, toads, vipers, etc., are noxious to the body, and poison the sensitive life; these poison the soul, corrupt our posterity, ensnare our children, destroy the vitals of our happiness, our future felicity, and contaminate the whole mass.

Shall any law be given to such wild creatures? Some beasts are for sport, and the huntsmen give them advantages of ground; but some are knocked on the head by all possible ways of violence and surprise.

I do not prescribe fire and faggot, but, as Scipio said of Carthage, *Delenda est Carthago*. They are to be rooted out of this nation, if ever we will live in peace, serve God, or enjoy our own. As for the manner, I leave it to those hands who have a right to execute God's justice on the nation's and the Church's enemies.

But if we must be frighted from this justice under the specious pretences and odious sense of cruelty, nothing will be effected : it will be more barbarous to our own children and dear posterity when they shall reproach their fathers, as we do ours, and tell us, 'You had an opportunity to root out this cursed race from the world under the favour and protection of a true English queen ; and out of your foolish pity you spared them, because, forsooth, you would not be cruel ; and now our Church is suppressed and persecuted, our religion trampled under foot, our estates plundered, our persons imprisoned and dragged to jails, gibbets, and scaffolds : your sparing this Amalekite race is our destruction, your mercy to them proves cruelty to your poor posterity.'

How just will such reflections be when our posterity shall fall under the merciless clutches of this uncharitable generation, when our Church shall be swallowed up in schism, faction, enthusiasm, and confusion ; when our Government shall be devolved upon foreigners, and our monarchy dwindled into a republic.

It would be more rational for us, if we must spare this generation, to summon our own to a general massacre, and as we have brought them into the world free, send them out so, and not betray them to destruction by our supine negligence, and then cry, 'It is mercy.'

Moses was a merciful, meek man, and yet with what fury did he run through the camp, and cut the throats of three and thirty thousand of his dear Israelites that were fallen into idolatry. What was the reason? It was mercy to the rest to make these examples, to prevent the destruction of the whole army.

How many millions of future souls we save from infection and delusion if the present race of poisoned spirits were purged from the face of the land!

It is vain to trifle in this matter, the light, foolish handling of them by mulcts, fines, etc.,—it is their glory and their advantage. If the gallows instead of the Counter, and the galleys instead of the fines, were the reward of going to a conventicle, to preach or hear, there would not be so many sufferers. The spirit of martyrdom is over; they that will go to church to be chosen sheriffs and mayors would go to forty churches rather than be hanged.

If one severe law were made and punctually executed, that whoever was found at a conventicle should be banished the nation and the preacher be anged, we should soon see an end of the tale. They would all come to church, and one age would make us all one again.

To talk of five shillings a month for not coming to the sacrament, and one shilling per week for not coming to church, this is such a way of converting

people as never was known ; this is selling them a
liberty to transgress for so much money. If it be not
a crime, why don't we give them full license ? And
if it be, no price ought to compound for the committing it, for that is selling a liberty to people to
sin against God and the Government.

If it be a crime of the highest consequence both
against the peace and welfare of the nation, the glory
of God, the good of the Church, and the happiness
of the soul, let us rank it among capital offences, and
let it receive a punishment in proportion to it.

We hang men for trifles, and banish them for
things not worth naming ; but an offence against God
and the Church, against the welfare of the world and
the dignity of religion, shall be bought off for five
shillings ! This is such a shame to a Christian
Government that it is with regret I transmit it to
posterity.

If men sin against God, affront His ordinances,
rebel against His Church, and disobey the precepts
of their superiors, let them suffer as such capital
crimes deserve. So will religion flourish, and this
divided nation be once again united.

And yet the title of barbarous and cruel will
soon be taken off from this law too. I am not supposing that all the Dissenters in England should be
hanged or banished, but, as in cases of rebellions
and insurrections, if a few of the ringleaders suffer,

the multitude are dismissed; so, a few obstinate
people being made examples, there is no doubt but
the severity of the law would find a stop in the compliance of the multitude.

To make the reasonableness of this matter out of
question, and more unanswerably plain, let us examine
for what it is that this nation is divided into parties
and factions, and let us see how they can justify a
separation, or we of the Church of England can
justify our bearing the insults and inconveniences of
the party.

One of their leading pastors, and a man of as
much learning as most among them, in his answer to
a pamphlet, entitled 'An Inquiry into the Occasional
Conformity,' has these words, p. 27, 'Do the religion
of the Church and the meeting-houses make two religions? Wherein do they differ? The substance of
the same religion is common to them both; and the
modes and accidents are the things in which only
they differ.' P. 28: 'Thirty-nine articles are given
us for the summary of our religion; thirty-six contain
the substance of it, wherein we agree; three the
additional appendices, about which we have some
differences.'

Now, if, as by their own acknowledgment, the
Church of England is a true Church, and the difference between them is only in a few modes and
accidents, why should we expect that they will suffer

galleys, corporeal punishment, and banishment for these trifles? There is no question but they will be wiser; even their own principles will not bear them out in it; they will certainly comply with the laws and with reason; and though at the first severity they may seem hard, the next age will feel nothing of it; the contagion will be rooted out; the disease being cured, there will be no need of the operation; but if they should venture to transgress and fall into the pit, all the world must condemn their obstinacy, as being without ground from their own principles.

Thus the pretence of cruelty will be taken off, and the party actually suppressed, and the disquiets they have so often brought upon the nation prevented.

Their numbers and their wealth make them haughty, and that is so far from being an argument to persuade us to forbear them, that it is a warning to us, without any delay, to reconcile them to the unity of the Church or remove them from us.

At present, Heaven be praised, they are not so formidable as they have been, and it is our own fault if ever we suffer them to be so. Providence and the Church of England seem to join in this particular, that now the destroyers of the nation's peace may be overturned, and to this end the present opportunity seems to be put into our hands.

To this end her present Majesty seems reserved to enjoy the crown, that the ecclesiastic as well as civil rights of the nation may be restored by her hand. To this end the face of affairs have received such a turn in the process of a few months as never has been before ; the leading men of the nation, the universal cry of the people, the unanimous request of the clergy, agree in this, that the deliverance of our Church is at hand. For this end has Providence given us such a Parliament, such a Convocation, such a gentry, and such a Queen as we never had before. And what may be the consequences of a neglect of such opportunities ? The succession of the crown has but a dark prospect; another Dutch turn may make the hopes of it ridiculous and the practice impossible. Be the house of our future princes never so well inclined, they will be foreigners, and many years will be spent in suiting the genius of strangers to this crown and the interests of the nation ; and how many ages it may be before the English throne be filled with so much zeal and candour, so much tenderness and hearty affection to the Church as we see it now covered with, who can imagine ?

It is high time, then, for the friends of the Church of England to think of building up and establishing her in such a manner that she may be no more invaded by foreigners nor divided by factions, schisms, and error.

If this could be done by gentle and easy methods, I should be glad ; but the wound is corroded, the vitals begin to mortify, and nothing but amputation of members can complete the cure ; all the ways of tenderness and compassion, all persuasive arguments, have been made use of in vain.

The humour of the Dissenters has so increased among the people that they hold the Church in defiance, and the house of God is an abomination among them ; nay, they have brought up their posterity in such prepossessed aversions to our holy religion that the ignorant mob think we are all idolaters and worshippers of Baal, and account it a sin to come within the walls of our churches.

The primitive Christians were not more shy of a heathen temple or of meat offered to idols, nor the Jews of swine's flesh, than some of our Dissenters are of the Church, and the divine service selemnised therein.

This obstinacy must be rooted out with the profession of it ; while the generation are less at liberty daily to affront God Almighty and dishonour His holy worship, we are wanting in our duty to God and our mother, the Church of England.

How can we answer it to God, to the Church, and to our posterity, to leave them entangled with fanaticism, error, and obstinacy in the bowels of the nation ; to leave them an enemy in their streets, that in time may involve them in the same crimes, and endanger the utter extirpation of religion in the nation ?

What is the difference betwixt this and being subjected to the power of the Church of Rome, from whence we have reformed? If one be an extreme on one hand, and one on another, it is equally destructive to the truth to have errors settled among us, let them be of what nature they will.

Both are enemies of our Church and of our peace; and why should it not be as criminal to admit an enthusiast as a Jesuit? Why should the Papist with his seven sacraments be worse than the Quaker with no sacraments at all? Why should religious houses be more intolerable than meeting-houses? Alas, the Church of England! What with Popery on one hand, and schismatics on the other, how has she been crucified between two thieves!

Now let us crucify the thieves. Let her foundations be established upon the destruction of her enemies. The doors of mercy being always open to the returning part of the deluded people, let the obstinate be ruled with the rod of iron.

Let all true sons of so holy and oppressed a mother, exasperated by her afflictions, harden their hearts against those who have oppressed her.

And may God Almighty put it into the hearts of all the friends of truth to lift up a standard against pride and Antichrist, that the posterity of the sons of error may be rooted out from the face of this land, for ever.

III.—THE 'DRAPIER'S LETTERS'

(Nos. 1 and 2)

By Jonathan Swift

(*The two pamphlets entitled* The Conduct of the Allies *and* The Public Spirit of the Whigs—*which are sometimes considered the capital examples of the political efforts of Swift's magnificent genius—were the very Jachin and Boaz of the Tory administration in the last years of Anne, and the effect of them has been admitted by such a violent Whig and such a good critic as Jeffrey. They seemed, however, not wholly suitable for insertion here ; first, because of their length (for one would have occupied nearly a third, the other nearly a fourth of this volume), and secondly, because the greater part of each does really, to some extent, underlie the charge brought against political pamphlets generally, and, being occupied with a great number of personal and particular matters, requires either much intimacy with the period or elaborate and probably tedious comparison and elucidation, to make it intelligible. No such drawback attaches*

to the almost more famous Drapier's Letters, *of which
I give the first and second.　They were written at
the very zenith of their author's marvellous powers,
and at the time when his* sæva indignatio *was heated
seven times hotter than usual by the conviction that his
last hope of English promotion was gone.　Their circumstances are simple and well known.　Wood had
received a patent to coin copper money for Ireland to the
amount of £*108,000.　*Most commentators seem to
think that he would have done this honestly enough ; to
me the simple fact that on the revocation of his patent a
pension of £*3000 *a year was given to him in compensation is proof enough of the contrary.　It is impossible
to imagine any honest profit on a transaction of such a
nature to such an amount which could rise to the
capital value of such a pension.　That Swift was
instigated to take up his pen against the transaction by
private griefs against the Ministry is extremely probable ;
that the thing was not a job less so.　As before, I must
refer to biographers for the details of the matter ; the
text is what interests us here.　I shall only remind the
reader that Swift was fifty-seven when the ' Drapier '
wrote, that* Gulliver *appeared about three years later,
and that Swift himself expired—lunatic and miserable
beyond utterance—on the* 19th October 1745, *twenty-one
years after all Dublin and half England had rung
with the boldness and the triumph of the ' Drapier.'*)

I

To the Tradesmen, Shop-Keepers, Farmers, and Common-People in general, of the Kingdom of Ireland; concerning the Brass Half-pence coined by Mr. Wood.

BRETHREN, FRIENDS, COUNTRYMEN, AND FELLOW SUBJECTS—What I intend now to say to you, is, next to your duty to God, and the care of your salvation, of the greatest concern to yourselves, and your children; your bread and clothing, and every common necessary of life entirely depend upon it. Therefore I do most earnestly exhort you as men, as Christians, as parents, and as lovers of your country, to read this paper with the utmost attention, or get it read to you by others; which that you may do at the less expence, I have ordered the printer to sell it at the lowest rate.

It is a great fault among you, that when a person writes with no other intention than to do you good you will not be at the pains to read his advices: one copy of this paper may serve a dozen of you, which will be less than a farthing a-piece. It is your folly that you have no common or general interest in your view, not even the wisest among you, neither do you know or enquire, or care who are your friends or who are your enemies.

E

About four years ago, a little book was written, to advise all people to wear the manufactures of this our own dear country : it had no other design, said nothing against the king or Parliament, or any man, yet the poor printer was prosecuted two years, with the utmost violence, and even some weavers themselves, for whose sake it was written, being upon the jury, found him guilty. This would be enough to discourage any man from endeavouring to do you good, when you will either neglect him or fly in his face for his pains, and when he must expect only danger to himself and loss of money, perhaps to his ruin.

However, I cannot but warn you once more of the manifest destruction before your eyes, if you do not behave yourselves as you ought.

I will therefore first tell you the plain story of the fact ; and then I will lay before you how you ought to act in common prudence, and according to the laws of your country.

The fact is thus, It having been many years since copper half-pence or farthings were last coined in this kingdom, they have been for some time very scarce, and many counterfeits passed about under the name of raps. Several applications were made to England, that we might have liberty to coin new ones, as in former times we did ; but they did not succeed. At last one Mr Wood a mean ordinary man, a hard-ware dealer, procured a patent under his Majesty's Broad Seal to coin fourscore and ten thousand pounds in copper for this kingdom, which patent however did not oblige any one here to take them, unless they pleased. Now you must know, that the half-pence and farthings in England pass for very little more than they are worth. And if you should beat them to pieces, and sell them to the brazier, you would not lose above a penny in a shilling. But Mr. Wood made his half-pence of such base metal, and so much smaller than the English ones, that the brazier would not give you above a penny of good money for a shilling of his; so that this sum of fourscore and ten thousand pounds in good gold and silver, must be given for trash that will not be worth above eight or nine thousand pounds real value. But this is not the worst, for Mr. Wood, when he pleases, may by stealth send over another and another fourscore and ten thousand pounds, and buy all our goods for eleven parts in twelve, under the value. For example, if a hatter sells a dozen of hats for five shillings a-piece, which amounts to three pounds, and receives the payment in Mr. Wood's coin, he really receives only the value of five shillings.

Perhaps you will wonder how such an ordinary fellow as this Mr. Wood could have so much interest as to get his Majesty's Broad Seal for so great a sum of bad money to be sent to this poor country, and

that all the nobility and gentry here could not obtain
the same favour, and let us make our own half-pence,
as we used to do.   Now I will make that matter very
plain.   We are at a great distance from the king's
court, and have nobody there to solicit for us, although a great number of lords and squires, whose
estates are here, and are our countrymen, spend all
their lives and fortunes there.   But this same Mr.
Wood was able to attend constantly for his own
interest; he is an Englishman and had great friends,
and it seems knew very well where to give money to
those that would speak to others that could speak to
the king and could tell a fair story.   And his
majesty, and perhaps the great lord or lords who
advised him, might think it was for our country's good;
and so, as the lawyers express it, the king was
deceived in his grant, which often happens in all
reigns.   And I am sure if his majesty knew that such
a patent, if it should take effect according to the
desire of Mr. Wood, would utterly ruin this kingdom,
which hath given such great proofs of its loyalty, he
would immediately recall it, and perhaps show his
displeasure to somebody or other: but a word to
the wise is enough.   Most of you must have heard,
with what anger our honourable House of Commons
receiv'd an account of this Wood's patent.   There
were several fine speeches made upon it, and plain
proofs that it was all a wicked cheat from the bottom

to the top, and several smart votes were printed, which that same Wood had the assurance to answer likewise in print, and in so confident a way, as if he were a better man than our whole Parliament put together.

This Wood, as soon as his patent was passed, or soon after, sends over a great many barrels of those half-pence, to Cork and other seaport towns, and to get them off, offered an hundred pounds in his coin for seventy or eighty in silver : but the collectors of the king's customs very honestly refused to take them, and so did almost everybody else. And since the Parliament hath condemned them, and desired the king that they might be stopped, all the kingdom do abominate them.

But Wood is still working under hand to force his half-pence upon us, and if he can by help of his friends in England prevail so far as to get an order that the commissioners and collectors of the king's money shall receive them, and that the army is to be paid with them, then he thinks his work shall be done. And this is the difficulty you will be under in such a case : for the common soldier when he goes to the market or ale-house will offer this money, and if it be refused, perhaps he will swagger and hector, and threaten to beat the butcher or ale-wife, or take the goods by force, and throw them the bad half-pence. In this and the like cases the shop-keeper, or victualler, or any other tradesman, has no more to do than to demand ten times the price of his goods if it is to be paid in Wood's money; for example, twenty pence of that money for a quart of ale, and so in all things else, and not part with his goods till he gets the money.

For suppose you go to an ale-house with that base money, and the landlord gives you a quart for four of these half-pence, what must the victualler do? His brewer will not be paid in that coin, or if the brewer should be such a fool, the farmers will not take it from them for their bere, because they are bound by their leases to pay their rents in good and lawful money of England, which this is not, nor of Ireland neither, and the Squire their landlord will never be so bewitched to take such trash for his land; so that it must certainly stop somewhere or other, and where-ever it stops it is the same thing, and we are all undone.

The common weight of these half-pence is between four and five to an ounce; suppose five, then three shillings and fourpence will weigh a pound, and conse-quently twenty shillings will weigh six pounds butter weight. Now there are many hundred farmers who pay two hundred pound a year rent. Therefore when one of these farmers comes with his half year's rent, which is one hundred pound, it will be at least six hundred pound weight, which is three horses load.

If a squire has a mind to come to town to buy

clothes and wine and spices for himself and family, or perhaps to pass the winter here, he must bring with him five or six horses loaden with sacks as the farmers bring their corn ; and when his lady comes in her coach to our shops, it must be followed by a car loaded with Mr. Wood's money. And I hope we shall have the grace to take it for no more than it is worth.

They say Squire Conolly has sixteen thousand pounds a year ; now if he sends for his rent to town, as it is likely he does, he must have two hundred and fifty horses to bring up his half-year's rent, and two or three great cellars in his house for stowage. But what the bankers will do I cannot tell. For I am assured that some great bankers keep by them forty thousand pounds in ready cash, to answer all payments, which sum, in Mr. Wood's money, would require twelve hundred horses to carry it.

For my own part, I am already resolved what to do ; I have a pretty good shop of Irish stuffs and silks, and instead of taking Mr. Wood's bad copper, I intend to truck with my neighbours the butchers, and bakers, and brewers, and the rest, goods for goods, and the little gold and silver I have I will keep by me like my heart's blood till better times, or till I am just ready to starve, and then I will buy Mr. Wood's money, as my father did the brass money in K. James's time, who could buy ten pound of it with a guinea, and I hope to get as much for a pistole, and so purchase bread from those who will be such fools as to sell it me.

These half-pence, if they once pass, will soon be counterfeit, because it may be cheaply done, the stuff is so base. The Dutch likewise will probably do the same thing, and send them over to us to pay for our goods; and Mr. Wood will never be at rest but coin on : so that in some years we shall have at least five times fourscore and ten thousand pounds of this lumber. Now the current money of this kingdom is not reckoned to be above four hundred thousand pounds in all; and while there is a silver sixpence left, these blood-suckers will never be quiet.

When once the kingdom is reduced to such a condition I will tell you what must be the end: the gentlemen of estates will all turn off their tenants for want of payment, because, as I told you before, the tenants are obliged by their leases to pay sterling, which is lawful current money of England; then they will turn their own farmers, as too many of them do already, run all into sheep where they can, keeping only such other cattle as are necessary; then they will be their own merchants, and send their wool and butter and hides and linen beyond sea for ready money and wine and spices and silks. They will keep only a few miserable cottiers. The farmers must rob or beg, or leave their country. The shop-keepers in this and every other town must break and starve : for it is the landed man that maintains the merchant, and shop-keeper, and handicraftsman.

But when the squire turns farmer and merchant himself, all the good money he gets from abroad he will hoard up to send for England, and keep some poor tailor or weaver and the like in his own house, who will be glad to get bread at any rate.

I should never have done, if I were to tell you all the miseries that we shall undergo if we be so foolish and wicked as to take this cursed coin. It would be very hard if all Ireland should be put into one scale, and this sorry fellow Wood into the other, that Mr. Wood should weigh down this whole kingdom, by which England gets above a million of good money every year clear into their pockets, and that is more than the English do by all the world besides.

But your great comfort is, that, as his majesty's patent does not oblige you to take this money, so the laws have not given the Crown a power of forcing the subjects to take what money the king pleases : for then, by the same reason, we might be bound to take pebble-stones or cockle-shells, or stamped leather for current coin, if ever we should happen to live under an ill prince, who might likewise by the same power make a guinea pass for ten pounds, a shilling for twenty shillings, and so on, by which he would in a short time get all the silver and gold of the kingdom into his own hands, and leave us nothing but brass or leather or what he pleased. Neither is anything reckoned more cruel or oppressive in the French Government than their common practice of calling in all their money after they have sunk it very low, and then coining it a-new at a much higher value, which however is not the thousandth part so wicked as this abominable project of Mr. Wood. For the French give their subjects silver for silver, and gold for gold ; but this fellow will not so much as give us good brass or copper for our gold and silver, nor even a twelfth part of their worth.

Having said this much, I will now go on to tell you the judgments of some great lawyers in this matter, whom I fee'd on purpose for your sakes, and got their opinions under their hands, that I might be sure I went upon good grounds.

A famous law-book call'd the *Mirrour of Justice*, discoursing of the articles (or laws) ordained by our ancient kings, declares the law to be as follows : It was ordained that no king of this realm should change, impair, or amend the money or make any other money than of gold or silver without the assent of all the counties, that is, as my Lord Coke says, without the assent of Parliament.

This book is very ancient, and of great authority for the time in which it was wrote, and with that character is often quoted by that great lawyer my

Lord Coke. By the laws of England, several metals are divided into lawful or true metal and unlawful or false metal; the former comprehends silver or gold, the latter all baser metals: that the former is only to pass in payments appears by an Act of Parliament made the twentieth year of Edward the First, called the statute concerning the passing of pence, which I give you here as I got it translated into English; for some of our laws at that time were, as I am told, writ in Latin: Whoever in buying or selling presumeth to refuse an half-penny or farthing of lawful money, bearing the stamp which it ought to have, let him be seized on as a contemner of the king's majesty, and cast to prison.

By this statute, no person is to be reckoned a contemner of the king's majesty, and for that crime to be committed to prison, but he who refuses to accept the king's coin made of lawful metal, by which, as I observ'd before, silver and gold only are intended.

That this is the true construction of the Act, appears not only from the plain meaning of the words, but from my Lord Coke's observation upon it. By this Act (says he) it appears that no subject can be forc'd to take in buying or selling or other payments, any money made but of lawful metal; that is, of silver or gold.

The law of England gives the king all mines of

gold and silver, but not the mines of other metals; the reason of which prerogative or power, as it is given by my Lord Coke, is, because money can be made of gold and silver, but not of other metals.

Pursuant to this opinion half-pence and farthings were anciently made of silver, which is more evident from the Act of Parliament of Henry the IVth. chap. 4, by which it is enacted as follows : Item, for the great scarcity that is at present within the realm of England of half-pence and farthings of silver, it is ordained and established that the third part of all the money of silver plate which shall be brought to the bullion, shall be made in half-pence and farthings. This shows that by the words half-penny and farthing of lawful money in that statute concerning the passing of pence, is meant a small coin in half-pence and farthings of silver.

This is further manifest from the statute of the ninth year of Edward the IIId. chap. 3, which enacts, That no sterling half-penny or farthing be molten for to make vessel, or any other thing by the goldsmiths, nor others, upon forfeiture of the money so molten (or melted).

By another Act in this king's reign black money was not to be current in England, and by an Act made in the eleventh year of his reign, chap. 5, galley half-pence were not to pass: what kind of coin these were I do not know, but I presume they were made of base metal, and that these Acts were no new laws, but further declarations of the old laws relating to the coin.

Thus the law stands in relation to coin, nor is there any example to the contrary, except one in Davis's *Reports*, who tells us, that in the time of Tyrone's rebellion Queen Elizabeth ordered money of mixt metal to be coined in the Tower of London, and sent over hither for payment of the army, obliging all people to receive it, and commanding that all silver money should be taken only as bullion, that is, for as much as it weighed. Davis tells us several particulars in this matter too long here to trouble you with, and that the Privy Council of this kingdom obliged a merchant in England to receive this mixt money for goods transmitted hither.

But this proceeding is rejected by all the best lawyers as contrary to law, the Privy Council here having no such power. And, besides, it is to be considered that the Queen was then under great difficulties by a rebellion in this kingdom, assisted from Spain, and whatever is done in great exigences and dangerous times should never be an example to proceed by in seasons of peace and quietness.

I will now, my dear friends, to save you the trouble, set before you, in short, what the law obliges you to do, and what it does not oblige you to.

First, You are oblig'd to take all money in

payments which is coin'd by the king and is of the English standard or weight, provided it be of gold or silver.

Secondly, You are not oblig'd to take any money which is not of gold or silver, not only the half-pence or farthings of England, or of any other country ; and it is only for convenience, or ease, that you are content to take them, because the custom of coining silver half-pence and farthings hath long been left off, I will suppose on account of their being subject to be lost.

Thirdly, Much less are we oblig'd to take those vile half-pence of that same Wood, by which you must lose almost eleven-pence in every shilling.

Therefore, my friends, stand to it one and all, refuse this filthy trash : it is no treason to rebel against Mr. Wood ; his majesty in his patent obliges nobody to take these half-pence ; our gracious prince hath no so ill advisers about him ; or if he had, yet you see the laws have not left it in the king's power, to force us to take any coin but what is lawful, of right standard, gold and silver ; therefore you have nothing to fear.

And let me in the next place apply myself particularly to you who are the poor sort of tradesmen : perhaps you may think you will not be so great losers as the rich if these half-pence should pass, because you seldom see any silver, and your customers come to your shops or stalls with nothing but brass,

which you likewise find hard to be got; but you may
take my word, whenever this money gains footing
among you, you will be utterly undone; if you carry
these half-pence to a shop for tobacco or brandy, or
any other thing you want, the shop-keeper will advance
his goods accordingly, or else he must break and
leave the key under the door. Do you think I will
sell you a yard of tenpenny stuff for twenty of Mr.
Wood's half-pence? No, not under two hundred at
least, neither will I be at the trouble of counting, but
weigh them in a lump. I will tell you one thing
further, that if Mr. Wood's project should take it will
ruin even our beggars: for when I give a beggar
an half-penny, it will quench his thirst, or go a good
way to fill his belly; but the twelfth part of a half-
penny will do him no more service than if I should
give him three pins out of my sleeve.

In short those half-pence are like the accursed
thing, which, as the Scripture tells us, the children of
Israel were forbidden to touch; they will run about
like the plague and destroy every one who lays his
hands upon them. I have heard scholars talk of a
man who told a king that he had invented a way to
torment people by putting them into a bull of brass
with fire under it, but the prince put the projector
first into his own brazen bull to make the experiment;
this very much resembles the project of Mr. Wood;
and the like of this may possibly be Mr. Wood's fate,

that the brass he contrived to torment this kingdom with, may prove his own torment, and his destruction at last.

N.B.—The author of this paper is inform'd by persons who have made it their business to be exact in their observations on the true value of these half-pence, that any person may expect to get a quart of twopenny ale for thirty-six of them.

I desire all persons may keep this paper carefully by them to refresh their memories whenever they shall have further notice of Mr. Wood's half-pence or any other the like imposture.

II

A LETTER TO MR. HARDING THE PRINTER, UPON OCCASION OF A PARAGRAPH IN HIS NEWS-PAPER OF AUGUST 1, 1724, RELATING TO MR. WOOD'S HALF-PENCE.

In your news-letter of the first instant there is a paragraph dated from London, July 25th, relating to Wood's half-pence ; whereby it is plain, what I fore-told in my letter to the shop-keepers, etc., that this vile fellow would never be at rest, and that the danger of our ruin approaches nearer, and therefore the kingdom requires new and fresh warning ; however I take that paragraph to be, in a great measure, an

imposition upon the public, at least I hope so,
because I am informed that Wood is generally his
own news-writer. I cannot but observe from that
paragraph that this public enemy of ours, not
satisfied to ruin us with his trash, takes every
occasion to treat this kingdom with the utmost contempt. He represents several of our merchants and
traders upon examination before a committee of a
council, agreeing that there was the utmost necessity
of copper-money here, before his patent, so that
several gentlemen have been forced to tally with their
workmen, and give them bits of cards sealed and
subscribed with their names. What then? If a
physician prescribe to a patient a dram of physic,
shall a rascal apothecary cram him with a pound, and
mix it up with poison? And is not a landlord's hand
and seal to his own labourers a better security for
five or ten shillings, than Wood's brass seven times
below the real value, can be to the kingdom, for an
hundred and four thousand pounds?

But who are these merchants and traders of
Ireland that make this report of the utmost necessity
we are under of copper money? They are only a few
betrayers of their country, confederates with Wood,
from whom they are to purchase a great quantity of
his coin, perhaps at half value, and vend it among us
to the ruin of the public and their own private
advantage. Are not these excellent witnesses, upon

whose integrity the fate of a kingdom must depend, who are evidences in their own cause, and sharers in this work of iniquity?

If we could have deserved the liberty of coining for ourselves, as we formerly did (and why we have not is everybody's wonder as well as mine), ten thousand pounds might have been coined here in Dublin of only one fifth below the intrinsic value, and this sum, with the stock of half-pence we then had, would have been sufficient: but Wood by his emissaries, enemies to God and this kingdom, hath taken care to buy up as many of our old half-pence as he could, and from thence the present want of change arises; to remove which, by Mr. Wood's remedy, would be, to cure a scratch on the finger by cutting off the arm. But supposing there were not one farthing of change in the whole nation, I will maintain that five and twenty thousand pounds would be a sum fully sufficient to answer all our occasions. I am no inconsiderable shop-keeper in this town, I have discoursed with several of my own and other trades, with many gentlemen both of city and country, and also with great numbers of farmers, cottagers, and labourers, who all agree that two shillings in change for every family would be more than necessary in all dealings. Now by the largest computation (even before that grievous discouragement of agriculture, which hath so much lessened our numbers) the souls in this kingdom are computed to be one million and a half, which, allowing but six to a family, makes two hundred and fifty thousand families, and consequently two shillings to each family will amount only to five and twenty thousand pounds, whereas this honest liberal hard-ware-man Wood, would impose upon us above four times that sum.

Your paragraph relates further, that Sir Isaac Newton reported an assay taken at the Tower, of Wood's metal, by which it appears that Wood had in all respects performed his contract. His contract! With whom? Was it with the Parliament or people of Ireland? Are not they to be the purchasers? But they detest, abhor, and reject it, as corrupt, fraudulent, mingled with dirt and trash. Upon which he grows angry, goes to law, and will impose his goods upon us by force.

But your news-letter says that an assay was made of the coin. How impudent and insupportable is this? Wood takes care to coin a dozen or two half-pence of good metal, sends them to the Tower and they are approved, and these must answer all that he hath already coined or shall coin for the future. It is true, indeed, that a gentleman often sends to my shop for a pattern of stuff, I cut it fairly off, and if he likes it he comes or sends and compares the pattern with the whole piece, and probably we come to a bargain. But if I were to buy an hundred sheep, and the grazier should bring me one single weather fat and well fleeced by way of pattern, and expect the same price round for the whole hundred, without suffering me to see them before he was paid, or giving me good security to restore my money for those that were lean or shorn or scabby, I would be none of his customer. I have heard of a man who had a mind to sell his house, and therefore carried a piece of brick in his pocket, which he showed as a pattern to encourage purchasers: and this is directly the case in point with Mr. Wood's assay.

The next part of the paragraph contains Mr. Wood's voluntary proposals for preventing any future objections or apprehensions.

His first proposal is, that whereas he hath already coined seventeen thousand pounds, and has copper prepared to make it up forty thousand pounds, he will be content to coin no more, unless the exigences of trade require it, though his patent empowers him to coin a far greater quantity.

To which if I were to answer it should be thus: Let Mr. Wood and his crew of founders and tinkers coin on till there is not an old kettle left in the kingdom; let them coin old leather, tobacco-pipe clay, or the dirt in the streets, and call their trumpery by what name they please from a guinea to a farthing, we are not under any concern to know how he and his tribe or accomplices think fit to employ themselves.

But I hope and trust that we are all to a man fully determined to have nothing to do with him or his ware.

The king has given him a patent to coin half-pence, but hath not obliged us to take them, and I have already shown in my Letter to the Shop-keepers, etc., that the law hath not left it in the power of the prerogative to compel the subject to take any money, beside gold and silver of the right sterling and standard.

Wood further proposes, (if I understand him right, for his expressions are dubious) that he will not coin above forty thousand pounds unless the exigences of trade require it: First, I observe that this sum of forty thousand pounds is almost double to what I proved to be sufficient for the whole kingdom, although we had not one of our old half-pence left. Again I ask, who is to be judge when the exigences of trade require it? Without doubt he means himself, for as to us of this poor kingdom, who must be utterly ruined if his project should succeed, we were never once consulted till the matter was over, and he will judge of our exigences by his own; neither will these be ever at an end till he and his accomplices will think they have enough: and it now appears that he will not be content with all our gold and silver, but intends to buy up our goods and manufactures with the same coin.

I shall not enter into examination of the prices for which he now proposes to sell his half-pence or what he calls his copper, by the pound; I have said enough of it in my former letter, and it hath likewise been considered by others. It is certain that, by his own first computation, we were to pay three shillings for what was intrinsically worth but one, although it had been of the true weight and standard for which he pretended to have contracted; but there is so great a difference both in weight and badness in several of his coins that some of them have been nine in ten below the intrinsic value, and most of them six or seven.

His last proposal being of a peculiar strain and nature, deserves to be very particularly consider'd, both on account of the matter and the style. It is as follows.

Lastly, in consideration of the direful apprehensions which prevail in Ireland, that Mr. Wood will by such coinage drain them of their gold and silver, he proposes to take their manufactures in exchange, and that no person be obliged to receive more than five-pence half-penny at one payment.

First, observe this little impudent hard-ware-man turning into ridicule the direful apprehensions of a whole kingdom, priding himself as the cause of them, and daring to prescribe what no king of England ever attempted, how far a whole nation shall be obliged to take his brass coin. And he has reason to insult ; for sure there was never an example in history of a great kingdom kept in awe for above a year in daily dread of utter destruction, not by a powerful invader at the head of twenty thousand men, not by a plague or a famine, not by a tyrannical prince (for we never had one more gracious) or a corrupt administration, but by one single, diminutive, insignificant, mechanic.

But to go on. To remove our direful apprehensions that he will drain us of our gold and silver by his coinage, this little arbitrary mock-monarch most graciously offers to take our manufactures in exchange. Are our Irish understandings indeed so low in his opinion? Is not this the very misery we complain of? That his cursed project will put us under the necessity of selling our goods for what is equal to nothing. How would such a proposal sound from France or Spain, or any other country we deal with, if they should offer to deal with us only upon this condition, that we should take their money at ten times higher than the intrinsic value? Does Mr. Wood think, for instance, that we will sell him a stone of wool for a parcel of his counters not worth sixpence, when we can send it to England and receive as many shillings in gold and silver? Surely there was never heard such a compound of impudence, villainy and folly.

His proposals conclude with perfect high-treason. He promises, that no person shall be obliged to receive more than five-pence half-penny of his coin in one payment : by which it is plain that he pretends to oblige every subject in this kingdom to take so much in every payment, if it be offered ; whereas his patent obliges no man, nor can the prerogative by law claim such a power, as I have often observed ; so that here Mr. Wood takes upon him the entire legislature, and an absolute dominion over the properties of the whole nation.

Good God ! Who are this wretch's advisers ? Who are his supporters, abettors, encouragers, or sharers ?   Mr. Wood will oblige me to take five-pence half-penny of his brass in every payment.   And I will shoot Mr. Wood and his deputies through the head, like highway-men or house-breakers, if they dare to force one farthing of their coin upon me in the payment of an hundred pounds.   It is no loss of honour to submit to the lion ; but who, with the figure of a man can think with patience of being devoured alive by a rat ?   He has laid a tax upon the people of Ireland of seventeen shillings at least in the pound ; a tax, I say, not only upon lands, but interest-money, goods, manufactures, the hire of handicraftsmen, labourers and servants.   Shop-keepers, look to yourselves.   Wood will oblige and force you to take five-pence half-penny of his trash in every payment, and many of you receive twenty, thirty, forty, payments in one day, or else you can hardly find bread : and pray consider how much that will amount to in a year; twenty times five-pence half-penny is nine shillings and two-pence, which is above an hundred and sixty pounds a year, whereof you will be losers of at least one hundred and forty pounds by taking your payments in his money. If any of you be con-tent to deal with Mr. Wood on such conditions they may. But for my own particular, let his money perish with him. If the famous Mr. Hampden rather chose to go to prison than pay a few shillings to King Charles I. without authority of Parliament, I will rather choose to be hanged than have all my substance taxed at seventeen shillings in the pound, at the arbitrary will and pleasure of the venerable Mr. Wood.

The paragraph concludes thus. *N.B.* (that is to say *nota bene*, or mark well) No evidence appeared from Ireland or elsewhere, to prove the mischiefs complained of, or any abuses whatsoever committed in the execution of the said grant.

The impudence of this remark exceeds all that went before. First, the House of Commons in Ireland, which represents the whole people of the kingdom ; and secondly the Privy Council, addressed his majesty against these half-pence. What could be done more to express the universal sense and opinion

of the nation ?   If his copper were diamonds, and the
kingdom were entirely against it, would not that be
sufficient to reject it?   Must a committee of the
House of Commons, and our whole Privy Council go
over to argue pro and con with Mr. Wood?   To
what end did the king give his patent for coining of
half-pence in Ireland?   Was it not, because it was
represented to his sacred majesty, that such a coinage
would be of advantage to the good of this kingdom,
and of all his subjects here?   It is to the patentee's
peril if his representation be false, and the execution
of his patent be fraudulent and corrupt.   Is he so
wicked and foolish to think that his patent was given
him to ruin a million and a half of people, that he
might be a gainer of three or fourscore thousand
pounds to himself?   Before he was at the charge of
passing a patent, much more of raking up so much
filthy dross, and stamping it with his majesty's image
and superscription, should he not first in common
sense, in common equity, and common manners, have
consulted the principal party concerned ; that is to
say, the people of the kingdom, the House of Lords
or Commons, or the Privy Council ?   If any foreigner
should ask us, whose image and superscription there
is on Wood's coin, we should be ashamed to tell him,
it was Cæsar's.   In that great want of copper half-
pence, which he alleges we were, our city set up our
Cæsar's statue in excellent copper, at an expence

that is equal in value to thirty thousand pounds of his coin ; and we will not receive his image in worse metal.

I observe many of our people putting a melancholy case on this subject. It is true say they, we are all undone if Wood's half-pence must pass; but what shall we do, if his majesty puts out a proclamation commanding us to take them ? This has been often dinned in my ears. But I desire my countrymen to be assured that there is nothing in it. The king never issues out a proclamation but to enjoin what the law permits him. He will not issue out a proclamation against law, or if such a thing should happen by a mistake, we are no more obliged to obey it than to run our heads into the fire. Besides, his majesty will never command us by a proclamation, what he does not offer to command us in the patent itself. There he leaves it to our discretion, so that our destruction must be entirely owing to ourselves. Therefore let no man be afraid of a proclamation, which will never be granted ; and if it should, yet upon this occasion, will be of no force. The king's revenues here are near four hundred thousand pounds a year, can you think his ministers will advise him to take them in Wood's brass, which will reduce the value to fifty thousand pounds ? England gets a million sterl. by this nation, which, if this project goes on, will be almost reduc'd to nothing : and do you think those who live in England upon Irish estates will be content to take an eighth or a tenth part, by being paid in Wood's dross?

If Wood and his confederates were not convinced of our stupidity, they never would have attempted so audacious an enterprise. He now sees a spirit hath been raised against him, and he only watches till it begins to flag, he goes about watching when to devour us. He hopes we shall be weary of contending with him, and at last out of ignorance, or fear, or of being perfectly tired with opposition, we shall be forced to yield. And therefore I confess it is my chief endeavour to keep up your spirits and resentments. If I tell you there is a precipice under you, and that if you go forwards you will certainly break your necks —if I point to it before your eyes, must I be at the trouble of repeating it every morning? Are our people's hearts waxed gross? Are their ears dull of hearing, and have they closed their eyes? I fear there are some few vipers among us, who, for ten or twenty pounds' gain, would sell their souls and their country, though at last it would end in their own ruin as well as ours. Be not like the deaf adder, who refuses to hear the voice of the charmer, charm he never so wisely.

Though my letter be directed to you, Mr. Harding, yet I intend it for all my countrymen. I have no interest in this affair but what is common to the public; I can live better than many others, I have some gold and silver by me, and a shop well furnished, and shall be able to make a shift when many of my betters are starving. But I am grieved to see the coldness and indifference of many people with whom I discourse. Some are afraid of a proclamation, others shrug up their shoulders, and cry, what would you have us to do? Some give out, there is no danger at all. Others are comforted that it will be a common calamity and they shall fare no worse than their neighbours. Will a man, who hears midnight-robbers at his door, get out of bed, and raise his family for a common defence, and shall a whole kingdom lie in a lethargy, while Mr. Wood comes at the head of his confederates to rob them of all they have, to ruin us and our posterity for ever? If an high-way-man meets you on the road, you give him your money to save your life ; but, God be thanked, Mr. Wood cannot touch a hair of your heads. You have all the laws of God and man on your side. When he or his accomplices offer you his dross, it is but saying No, and you are safe. If a madman should come to my shop with a handful of dirt raked out of the kennel, and offer it in payment for ten yards of stuff, I would pity or laugh at him, or, if his behaviour deserved it, kick him out of my doors. And if Mr. Wood comes to demand any gold or silver, or commodities for which I have paid my gold and silver, in exchange for his trash, can he deserve or expect better treatment?

When the evil day is come (if it must come) let us mark and observe those who presume to offer these half-pence in payment.   Let their names and trades, and places of abode be made public, that every one may be aware of them, as betrayers of their country, and confederates with Mr. Wood. Let them be watched at markets and fairs, and let the first honest discoverer give the word about, that Wood's half-pence have been offered, and caution the poor innocent people not to receive them.

Perhaps I have been too tedious ; but there would never be an end, if I attempt to say all that this melancholy subject will bear.   I will conclude with humbly offering one proposal, which if it were put in practice, would blow up this destructive project at once.   Let some skilful judicious pen draw up an advertisement to the following purpose :

Whereas one William Wood, hard-ware-man, now or lately sojourning in the city of London, hath, by many misrepresentations, procured a patent for coining an hundred and forty thousand pounds in copper half-pence for this kingdom, which is a sum five times greater than our occasions require : And whereas it is notorious that the said Wood hath coined his half-pence of such base metal and false weight, that they are, at least, six parts in seven below the real value : And whereas we have reason to apprehend that the said Wood may, at any time hereafter, clandestinely coin as many more half-pence as he pleases: And whereas the said patent neither doth nor can oblige his majesty's subjects to receive the said half-pence in any payment, but leaves it to their voluntary choice, because, by law the subject cannot be obliged to take any money except gold or silver: And whereas, contrary to the letter and meaning of the said patent, the said Wood hath declared that every person shall be obliged to take five-pence half-penny of his coin in every payment: And whereas the House of Commons and Privy Council have severally addressed his most sacred majesty representing the ill consequences which the said coinage may have upon this kingdom: And lastly, whereas it is universally agreed, that the whole nation to a man (except Mr. Wood and his confederates) are in the utmost apprehensions of the ruinous consequences that must follow from the said coinage. Therefore we, whose names are underwritten, being persons of considerable estates in this kingdom, and residers therein, do unanimously resolve and declare that we will never receive one farthing or half-penny of the said Wood's coining, and that we will direct all our tenants to refuse the said coin from any person whatsoever; of which, that they may not be ignorant, we have sent them a copy of this advertisement, to be read to them by our stewards, receivers, etc.

I could wish, that a paper of this nature might be

drawn up, and signed by two or three hundred principal gentlemen of this kingdom, and printed copies thereof sent to their several tenants; I am deceived, if anything could sooner defeat this execrable design of Wood and his accomplices. This would immediately give the alarm, and set the kingdom on their guard. This would give courage to the meanest tenant and cottager. *How long, O Lord, righteous and true,* etc.

I must tell you in particular, Mr. Harding, that you are much to blame. Several hundred persons have enquired at your house for my Letter to the Shop-keepers, etc., and you had none to sell them. Pray keep yourself provided with that letter and with this; you have got very well by the former, but I did not then write for your sake, any more than I do now. Pray advertise both in every news-paper, and let it not be your fault or mine if our countrymen will not take warning. I desire you likewise to sell them as cheap as you can.—I am your Servant,   M. B.

Aug. 4, 1724.

IV.—'SECOND LETTER ON A REGICIDE PEACE'

BY THE RIGHT HONOURABLE EDMUND BURKE

(I have found the selection of a suitable sample of Burke to be my most difficult task in this volume. All his writings, as I have pointed out in the general introduction, are, after a sort, pamphlets; and this of itself was an embarrassment. It was partly complicated and partly lessened by the fact that the form of his speeches naturally excluded them. Many of his other works—notably the Thoughts on the Present Discontents, *the immortal* Reflections on the French Revolution, *and the* Appeal from the New Whigs to the Old—*were much too long for a scheme in which I have made it a rule to give in each case entire works or divisions of works. I at last reduced the suitable candidates to three—the* Letter to Sir Hercules Langrishe, *that* To a Noble Lord, *and the present number of the* Letters on a Regicide Peace. *The first*

G

went as being to some extent identical in subject with the examples of another writer, Sydney Smith, which I had already resolved on giving; the second as being too much in the nature of a personal apologia. With the third, which I looked on at first with least favour, I have become increasingly well satisfied. It has not the gorgeous rhetoric of The Letter to a Noble Lord, *the* Reflections, *and others. It has nothing so lively as the contrast between France and Algiers in its immediate predecessor. It may even seem, to those who have accustomed themselves to think of Burke wholly or mainly as a gorgeous rhetorician, rather tame as a whole. But if it does not soar, it never droops; it is admirably proportioned, admirably written, and admirably argued throughout, and it shows great knowledge and mastery of foreign politics—the point in which English statesmen have always been weakest. I may add that it seems to me a triumphant refutation of the charge—constantly brought against Burke not merely by extreme democrats, but by the usual advocate of the* juste milieu,—*that in his later years, and especially in these very Letters, he became a mere raving Gallophobe, with no sense of proportion or circumstance. For my part, I have read scores, probably hundreds, of books—English, French, and German—on the French Revolution; I have never read one that made Burke obsolete. Let it only be added that the author, who was born in* 1730, *was very near the end of his career—he died next year—when*

he wrote these letters, and that the peace proposals which
he deprecated, and which he did not a little to avert,
were dictated on the one side by the sobering down of
the first Revolutionary fervour under the Directory; on
the other by the persistent ill-success of the Allies, and
the conflicts of interest and principle which had arisen
among them.)

My DEAR SIR—I closed my first letter with
serious matter, and I hope it has employed your
thoughts. The system of peace must have a re-
ference to the system of the war. On that ground,
I must therefore again recall your mind to our
original opinions, which time and events have not
taught me to vary.

My ideas and my principles led me, in this contest,
to encounter France, not as a state, but as a faction.
The vast territorial extent of that country, its immense
population, its riches of production, its riches of commerce and convention—the whole aggregate mass ot
what, in ordinary cases, constitutes the force of a
state, to me were but objects of secondary consideration. They might be balanced; and they have been
often more than balanced. Great as these things are,
they are not what make the faction formidable. It is
the faction that makes them truly dreadful. That
faction is the evil spirit that possesses the body of
France; that informs it as a soul; that stamps upon

its ambition, and upon all its pursuits, a characteristic mark, which strongly distinguishes them from the same general passions, and the same general views, in other men and in other communities. It is that spirit which inspires into them a new, a pernicious, a desolating activity. Constituted as France was ten years ago, it was not in that France to shake, to shatter, and to overwhelm Europe in the manner that we behold. A sure destruction impends over those infatuated princes, who, in the conflict with this new and unheard-of power, proceed as if they were engaged in a war that bore a resemblance to their former contests; or that they can make peace in the spirit of their former arrangements of pacification. Here the beaten path is the very reverse of the safe road.

As to me, I was always steadily of opinion, that this disorder was not in its nature intermittent. I conceived that the contest, once begun, could not be laid down again, to be resumed at our discretion; but that our first struggle with this evil would also be our last. I never thought we could make peace with the system; because it was not for the sake of an object we pursued in rivalry with each other, but with the system itself, that we were at war. As I understood the matter, we were at war not with its conduct, but with its existence; convinced that its existence and its hostility were the same.

The faction is not local or territorial. It is a general evil. Where it least appears in action, it is still full of life. In its sleep it recruits its strength, and prepares its exertion. Its spirit lies deep in the corruption of our common nature. The social order which restrains it, feeds it. It exists in every country in Europe ; and among all orders of men in every country, who look up to France as to a common head. The centre is there. The circumference is the world of Europe wherever the race of Europe may be settled. Everywhere else the faction is militant ; in France it is triumphant. In France it is the bank of deposit, and the bank of circulation, of all the pernicious principles that are forming in every state. It will be folly scarcely deserving of pity, and too mischievous for contempt, to think of restraining it in any other country whilst it is predominant there. War, instead of being the cause of its force, has suspended its operation. It has given a reprieve, at least, to the Christian world.

The true nature of a Jacobin war, in the beginning, was, by most of the Christian powers, felt, acknowledged, and even in the most precise manner declared. In the joint manifesto, published by the emperor and the king of Prussia, on the 4th of August, 1792, it is expressed in the clearest terms, and on principles which could not fail, if they had adhered to them, of classing those monarchs with the first benefactors of mankind. This manifesto was published, as they themselves express it, 'to lay open to the present generation, as well as to posterity, their motives, their intentions, and the *disinterestedness* of their personal views; taking up arms for the purpose of preserving social and political order amongst all civilised nations, and to secure to *each* state its religion, happiness, independence, territories, and real constitution.'—'On this ground, they hoped that all empires and all states would be unanimous; and becoming the firm guardians of the happiness of mankind, that they could not fail to unite their efforts to rescue a numerous nation from its own fury, to preserve Europe from the return of barbarism, and the universe from the subversion and anarchy with which it was threatened.' The whole of that noble performance ought to be read at the first meeting of any congress which may assemble for the purpose of pacification. In that piece 'these powers expressly renounce all views of personal aggrandisement,' and confine themselves to objects worthy of so generous, so heroic, and so perfectly wise and politic an enterprise. It was to the principles of this confederation, and to no other, that we wished our sovereign and our country to accede, as a part of the commonwealth of Europe. To these principles with some trifling exceptions and limitations they did fully accede. And all our friends who took office acceded to the ministry (whether wisely or not), as I always understood the matter, on the faith and on the principles of that declaration.

As long as these powers flattered themselves that the menace of force would produce the effect of force, they acted on those declarations : but when their menaces failed of success, their efforts took a new direction. It did not appear to them that virtue and heroism ought to be purchased by millions of rix-dollars. It is a dreadful truth, but it is a truth that cannot be concealed; in ability, in dexterity, in the distinctness of their views, the Jacobins are our superiors. They saw the thing right from the very beginning. Whatever were the first motives to the war among politicians, they saw that in its spirit, and for its objects, it was a *civil war*; and as such they pursued it. It is a war between the partisans of the ancient, civil, moral, and political order of Europe, against a sect of fanatical and ambitious atheists which means to change them all. It is not France extending a foreign empire over other nations ; it is a sect aiming at universal empire, and beginning with the conquest of France. The leaders of that sect secured the *centre of Europe*; and that secured, they knew, that whatever might be the event of battles and sieges, their *cause* was victorious. Whether its territory had a little more or a little less peeled from its surface, or whether an island or two was detached from its commerce, to them was of little moment.

The conquest of France was a glorious acquisition. That once well laid as a basis of empire, opportunities never could be wanting to regain or to replace what had been lost, and dreadfully to avenge themselves on the faction of their adversaries.

They saw it was a *civil war*. It was their business to persuade their adversaries that it ought to be a *foreign* war. The Jacobins everywhere set up a cry against the new crusade ; and they intrigued with effect in the cabinet, in the field, and in every private society in Europe. Their task was not difficult. The condition of princes, and sometimes of first ministers too, is to be pitied. The creatures of the desk, and the creatures of favour, had no relish for the principles of the manifestoes. They promised no governments, no regiments, no revenues from whence emoluments might arise by perquisite or by grant. In truth, the tribe of vulgar politicians are the lowest of our species. There is no trade so vile and mechanical as government in their hands. Virtue is not their habit. They are out of themselves in any course of conduct recommended only by conscience and glory. A large, liberal, and prospective view of the interests of states passes with them for romance ; and the principles that recommend it, for the wanderings of a disordered imagination. The calculators compute them out of their senses. The jesters and buffoons shame them out of everything grand and elevated.

Littleness in object and in means, to them appears soundness and sobriety. They think there is nothing worth pursuit but that which they can handle; which they can measure with a two-foot rule; which they can tell upon ten fingers.

Without the principles of the Jacobins, perhaps without any principles at all, they played the game of that faction. There was a beaten road before them. The powers of Europe were armed; France had always appeared dangerous; the war was easily diverted from France as a faction, to France as a state. The princes were easily taught to slide back into their old, habitual course of politics. They were easily led to consider the flames that were consuming France, not as a warning to protect their own buildings (which were without any party wall, and linked by a contignation into the edifice of France,) but as a happy occasion for pillaging the goods, and for carrying off the materials, of their neighbour's house. Their provident fears were changed into avaricious hopes. They carried on their new designs without seeming to abandon the principles of their old policy. They pretended to seek, or they flattered themselves that they sought, in the accession of new fortresses, and new territories, a *defensive* security. But the security wanted was against a kind of power which was not so truly dangerous in its fortresses nor in its territories, as in its spirit and its principles. The aimed, or pretended to aim, at *defending* themselves against a danger from which there can be no security in any *defensive* plan.   If armies and fortresses were a defence against Jacobinism, Louis the Sixteenth would this day reign a powerful monarch over a happy people.

This error obliged them, even in their offensive operations, to adopt a plan of war, against the success of which there was something little short of mathematical demonstration.   They refused to take any step which might strike at the heart of affairs.   They seemed unwilling to wound the enemy in any vital part.   They acted through the whole, as if they really wished the conservation of the Jacobin power, as what might be more favourable than the lawful government to the attainment of the petty objects they looked for.   They always kept on the circumference ; and the wider and remoter the circle was, the more eagerly they chose it as their sphere of action in this centrifugal war.   The plan they pursued, in its nature demanded great length of time.   In its execution, they, who went the nearest way to work, were obliged to cover an incredible extent of country. It left to the enemy every means of destroying this extended line of weakness.   Ill success in any part was sure to defeat the effect of the whole.   This is true of Austria.   It is still more true of England. On this false plan, even good fortune, by further weakening the victor, put him but the further off from his object.

As long as there was any appearance of success, the spirit of aggrandisement, and consequently the spirit of mutual jealousy, seized upon all the coalesced powers. Some sought an accession of territory at the expense of France, some at the expense of each other, some at the expense of third parties; and when the vicissitude of disaster took its turn, they found common distress a treacherous bond of faith and friendship.

The greatest skill conducting the greatest military apparatus has been employed; but it has been worse than uselessly employed, through the false policy of the war. The operations of the field suffered by the errors of the cabinet. If the same spirit continues when peace is made, the peace will fix and perpetuate all the errors of the war; because it will be made upon the same false principle. What has been lost in the field, in the field may be regained. An arrangement of peace in its nature is a permanent settlement; it is the effect of counsel and deliberation, and not of fortuitous events. If built upon a basis fundamentally erroneous, it can only be retrieved by some of those unforeseen dispensations, which the all-wise but mysterious Governor of the world some-times interposes, to snatch nations from ruin. It would not be pious error, but mad and impious presumption, for any one to trust in an unknown order of dispensations, in defiance of the rules of prudence, which are formed upon the known march of the ordinary providence of God.

It was not of that sort of war that I was amongst the least considerable, but amongst the most zealous advisers; and it is not by the sort of peace now talked of, that I wish it concluded. It would answer no great purpose to enter into the particular errors of the war. The whole has been but one error. It was but nominally a war of alliance. As the combined powers pursued it there was nothing to hold an alliance together. There could be no tie of *honour*, in a society for pillage. There could be no tie of a common *interest* where the object did not offer such a division amongst the parties as could well give them a warm concern in the gains of each other, or could indeed form such a body of equivalents, as might make one of them willing to abandon a separate object of his ambition for the gratification of any other member of the alliance. The partition of Poland offered an object of spoil in which the parties *might* agree. They were circumjacent, and each might take a portion convenient to his own territory. They might dispute about the value of their several shares, but the contiguity to each of the demandants always furnished the means of an adjustment. Though hereafter the world will have cause to rue this iniquitous

measure, and they most who were the most concerned in it, for the moment there was wherewithal
in the object to preserve peace amongst confederates
in wrong. But the spoil of France did not afford
the same facilities for accommodation. What might
satisfy the house of Austria in a Flemish frontier,
afforded no equivalent to tempt the cupidity of the
king of Prussia. What might be desired by Great
Britain in the West Indies, must be coldly and
remotely, if at all, felt as an interest at Vienna ; and
it would be felt as something worse than a negative
interest at Madrid. Austria, long possessed with
unwise and dangerous designs on Italy, could not be
very much in earnest about the conservation of the
old patrimony of the house of Savoy ; and Sardinia,
who owed to an Italian force all her means of shutting
out France from Italy, of which she has been supposed
to hold the key, would not purchase the means of
strength upon one side by yielding it on the other.
She would not readily give the possession of Nov-
ara for the hope of Savoy. No continental power
was willing to lose any of its continental objects for
the increase of the naval power of Great Britain ; and
Great Britain would not give up any of the objects
she sought for as the means of an increase to her
naval power, to further their aggrandisement.

The moment this war came to be considered as
a war merely of profit, the actual circumstances are

such that it never could become really a war of alliance. Nor can the peace be a peace of alliance, until things are put upon their right bottom.

I do not find it denied that when a treaty is entered into for peace, a demand will be made on the regicides to surrender a great part of their conquests on the continent. Will they, in the present state of the war, make that surrender without an equivalent? This continental cession must of course be made in favour of that party in the alliance that has suffered losses. That party has nothing to furnish towards an equivalent. What equivalent, for instance, has Holland to offer, who has lost her all? What equivalent can come from the Emperor, every part of whose territories contiguous to France is already within the pale of the regicide dominions? What equivalent has Sardinia to offer for Savoy and for Nice, I may say for her whole being? What has she taken from the faction of France? she has lost very near her all; and she has gained nothing. What equivalent has Spain to give? Alas! she has already paid for her own ransom the fund of equivalent, and a dreadful equivalent it is, to England and to herself. But I put Spain out of the question; she is a province of the Jacobin empire, and she must make peace or war according to the orders she receives from the directory of assassins. In effect and substance, her crown is a fief of regicide.

Whence then can the compensation be demanded? Undoubtedly from that power which alone has made some conquests. That power is England. Will the allies then give away their ancient patrimony, that England may keep islands in the West Indies? They never can protract the war in good earnest for that object; nor can they act in concert with us, in our refusal to grant anything towards their redemption. In that case we are thus situated. Either we must give Europe, bound hand and foot, to France; or we must quit the West Indies without any one object, great or small, towards indemnity and security. I repeat it, without any advantage whatever: because, supposing that our conquest could comprise all that France ever possessed in the tropical America, it never can amount in any fair estimation to a fair equivalent for Holland, for the Austrian Netherlands, for the lower Germany, that is, for the whole ancient kingdom or circle of Burgundy, now under the yoke of regicide, to say nothing of almost all Italy under the same barbarous domination. If we treat in the present situation of things, we have nothing in our hands that can redeem Europe. Nor is the Emperor, as I have observed, more rich in the fund of equivalents.

If we look to our stock in the eastern world, our most valuable and systematic acquisitions are made in that quarter. Is it from France they are made? France has but one or two contemptible factories, subsisting by the offal of the private fortunes ot English individuals to support them, in any part of India. I look on the taking of the Cape of Good Hope as the securing of a post of great moment. It does honour to those who planned, and to those who executed, that enterprise : but I speak of it always as comparatively good ; as good as anything can be in a scheme of war that repels us from a centre, and employs all our forces where nothing can be finally decisive. But giving, as I freely give, every possible credit to these eastern conquests, I ask one question, —on whom are they made? It is evident, that if we can keep our eastern conquests we keep them not at the expense of France, but at the expense of Holland our *ally* ; of Holland, the immediate cause of the war, the nation whom we had undertaken to protect, and not of the republic which it was our business to destroy. If we return the African and the Asiatic conquests, we put them into the hands of a nominal state (to that Holland is reduced) unable to retain them ; and which will virtually leave them under the direction of France. If we withhold them, Holland declines still more as a state. She loses so much carrying trade, and that means of keeping up the small degree of naval power she holds ; for which policy alone, and not for any commercial gain, she maintains the Cape, or any settlement beyond it. In that case, resentment, faction, and even necessity, will throw her more and more into the power of the new, mischievous republic. But on the probable state of Holland I shall say more, when in this correspondence I come to talk over with you the state in which any sort of Jacobin peace will leave all Europe.

So far as to the East Indies.

As to the West Indies, indeed as to either, if we look for matter of exchange in order to ransom Europe, it is easy to show that we have taken a terribly roundabout road. I cannot conceive, even if, for the sake of holding conquests there, we should refuse to redeem Holland, and the Austrian Netherlands, and the hither Germany, that Spain, merely as she is Spain, (and forgetting that the regicide ambassador governs at Madrid,) will see, with perfect satisfaction, Great Britain sole mistress of the isles. In truth it appears to me, that, when we come to balance our account, we shall find in the proposed peace only the pure, simple, and unendowed charms of Jacobin amity. We shall have the satisfaction of knowing, that no blood or treasure has been spared by the allies for support of the regicide system. We shall reflect at leisure on one great truth, that it was ten times more easy totally to destroy the system itself, than, when established, it would be to reduce its power; and that this republic, most formidable abroad, was of all things the weakest at home; that her frontier was terrible, her interior feeble; that it

H

was matter of choice to attack her where she is invincible, and to spare her where she was ready to dissolve by her own internal disorders.   We shall reflect, that our plan was good neither for offence nor defence.

It would not be at all difficult to prove, that an army of a hundred thousand men, horse, foot, and artillery, might have been employed against the enemy on the very soil which he has usurped, at a far less expense than has been squandered away upon tropical adventures.   In these adventures it was not an enemy we had to vanquish, but a cemetery to conquer.   In carrying on the war in the West Indies, the hostile sword is merciful ; the country in which we engage is the dreadful enemy.   There the European conqueror finds a cruel defeat in the very fruits of his success.   Every advantage is but a new demand on England for recruits to the West Indian grave. In a West India war, the regicides have, for their troops, a race of fierce barbarians, to whom the poisoned air, in which our youth inhale certain death, is salubrity and life.   To them the climate is the surest and most faithful of allies.

Had we carried on the war on the side of France which looks towards the Channel or the Atlantic, we should have attacked our enemy on his weak and unarmed side.   We should not have to reckon on the loss of a man who did not fall in battle.   We

should have an ally in the heart of the country, who,
to our hundred thousand, would at one time have
added eighty thousand men at the least, and all ani-
mated by principle, by enthusiasm, and by vengeance ;
motives which secured them to the cause in a very
different manner from some of those allies whom we
subsidised with millions.   This ally, (or rather this
principal in the war,) by the confession of the regicide
himself, was more formidable to him than all his
other foes united.   Warring there, we should have
led our arms to the capital of Wrong.   Defeated, we
could not fail (proper precautions taken) of a sure
retreat.   Stationary, and only supporting the royalists,
an impenetrable barrier, an impregnable rampart,
would have been formed between the enemy and his
naval power.   We are probably the only nation who
have declined to act against an enemy, when it might
have been done in his own country ; and who having
an armed, a powerful, and a long-victorious ally in
that country, declined all effectual co-operation, and
suffered him to perish for want of support.   On the
plan of a war in France, every advantage that our
allies might obtain would be doubled in its effect.
Disasters on the one side might have a fair chance of
being compensated by victories on the other.   Had
we brought the main of our force to bear upon that
quarter, all the operations of the British and Imperial
crowns would have been combined.   The war would

have had system, correspondence, and a certain direction. But as the war has been pursued, the operations of the two crowns have not the smallest degree of mutual bearing or relation.

Had acquisitions in the West Indies been our object, on success in France, everything reasonable in those remote parts might be demanded with decorum, and justice, and a sure effect. Well might we call for a recompence in America, for those services to which Europe owed its safety. Having abandoned this obvious policy connected with principle, we have seen the regicide power taking the reverse course, and making real conquests in the West Indies, to which all our dear-bought advantages (if we could hold them) are mean and contemptible. The noblest island within the tropics, worth all that we possess put together, is, by the vassal Spaniard, delivered into her hands. The island of Hispaniola (of which we have but one poor corner, by a slippery hold) is perhaps equal to England in extent, and in fertility is far superior. The part possessed by Spain, of that great island, made for the seat and centre of a tropical empire, was not improved, to be sure, as the French division had been, before it was systematically destroyed by the cannibal republic; but it is not only the far larger, but the far more salubrious and more fertile part.

It was delivered into the hands of the barbarians

without, as I can find, any public reclamation on our
part, not only in contravention to one of the fundamental treaties that compose the public law of Europe,
but in defiance of the fundamental colonial policy of
Spain herself. This part of the treaty of Utrecht was
made for great general ends unquestionably; but whilst
it provided for those general ends, it was in affirmance
of that particular policy. It was not to injure, but
to save Spain by making a settlement of her estate,
which prohibited her to alienate to France. It is
her policy not to see the balance of West Indian
power overturned by France or by Great Britain.
Whilst the monarchies subsisted, this unprincipled
cession was what the influence of the elder branch of
the house of Bourbon never dared to attempt on the
younger : but cannibal terror has been more powerful
than family influence. The Bourbon monarchy of
Spain is united to the republic of France, by what
may be truly called the ties of blood.

By this measure the balance of power in the West
Indies is totally destroyed. It has followed the
balance of power in Europe. It is not alone what
shall be left nominally to the assassins that is theirs.
Theirs is the whole empire of Spain in America.
That stroke finishes all. I should be glad to see our
suppliant negotiator in the act of putting his feather
to the ear of the directory, to make it unclinch the
fist ; and, by his tickling, to charm that rich prize out

of the iron gripe of robbery and ambition! It does
not require much sagacity to discern that no power
wholly baffled and defeated in Europe can flatter
itself with conquests in the West Indies. In that
state of things it can neither keep nor hold. No!
It cannot even long make war if the grand bank and
deposit of its force is at all in the West Indies. But
here a scene opens to my view too important to pass
by, perhaps too critical to touch. Is it possible that
it should not present itself in all its relations to a mind
habituated to consider either war or peace on a large
scale, or as one whole?

Unfortunately other ideas have prevailed. A
remote, an expensive, a murderous, and, in the end,
an unproductive adventure, carried on upon ideas of
mercantile knight-errantry, without any of the generous wildness of Quixotism, is considered as sound, solid
sense ; and a war in a wholesome climate, a war at
our door, a war directly on the enemy, a war in the
heart of his country, a war in concert with an internal
ally, and in combination with the external, is regarded
as folly and romance.

My dear friend, I hold it impossible that these
considerations should have escaped the statesmen on
both sides of the water, and on both sides of the
House of Commons. How a question of peace can
be discussed without having them in view, I cannot
imagine. If you or others see a way out of these

difficulties I am happy.   I see, indeed, a fund from whence equivalents will be proposed.   I see it.   But I cannot just now touch it.   It is a question of high moment.   It opens another Iliad of woes to Europe.

Such is the time proposed for making a *common political peace*, to which no one circumstance is propitious.   As to the grand principle of the peace, it is left, as if by common consent, wholly out of the question.

Viewing things in this light, I have frequently sunk into a degree of despondency and dejection hardly to be described ; yet out of the profoundest depths of this despair, an impulse, which I have in vain endeavoured to resist, has urged me to raise one feeble cry against this unfortunate coalition which is formed at home, in order to make a coalition with France, subversive of the whole ancient order of the world.   No disaster of war, no calamity of season, could ever strike me with half the horror which I felt from what is introduced to us by this junction of parties, under the soothing name of peace.   We are apt to speak of a low and pusillanimous spirit as the ordinary cause by which dubious wars terminated in humiliating treaties.   It is here the direct contrary. I am perfectly astonished at the boldness of character, at the intrepidity of mind, the firmness of nerve, in those who are able with deliberation to face the perils of Jacobin fraternity.

This fraternity is indeed so terrible in its nature, and in its manifest consequences, that there is no way of quieting our apprehensions about it, but by totally putting it out of sight, by substituting for it, through a sort of periphrasis, something of an ambiguous quality, and describing such a connexion under the terms of '*the usual relations of peace and amity.*' By this means the proposed fraternity is hustled in the crowd of those treaties, which imply no change in the public law of Europe, and which do not upon system affect the interior condition of nations. It is confounded with those conventions in which matters of dispute among sovereign powers are compromised, by the taking off a duty more or less, by the surrender of a frontier town, or a disputed district, on the one side or the other; by pactions in which the pretensions of families are settled, (as by a conveyancer, making family substitutions and successions,) without any alterations in the laws, manners, religion, privileges, and customs, of the cities, or territories, which are the subject of such arrangements.

All this body of old conventions, composing the vast and voluminous collection called the *corps diplomatique*, forms the code or statute law, as the methodised reasonings of the great publicists and jurists from the digest and jurisprudence of the Christian world. In these treasures are to be found the *usual* relations of peace and amity in civilised

Europe ; and there the relations of ancient France were to be found amongst the rest.

The present system in France is not the ancient France. It is not the ancient France with ordinary ambition and ordinary means. It is not a new power of an old kind. It is a new power of a new species. When such a questionable shape is to be admitted for the first time into the brotherhood of Christendom, it is not a mere matter of idle curiosity to consider how far it is in its nature alliable with the rest, or whether 'the relations of peace and amity' with this new state are likely to be of the same nature with the *usual* relations of the states of Europe.

The Revolution in France had the relation of France to other nations as one of its principal objects. The changes made by that Revolution were not the better to accommodate her to the old and usual relations, but to produce new ones. The Revolution was made, not to make France free, but to make her formidable ; not to make her a neighbour, but a mistress ; not to make her more observant of laws, but to put her in a condition to impose them. To make France truly formidable it was necessary that France should be new modelled. They, who have not followed the train of the late proceedings, have been led by deceitful representations (which deceit made a part in the plan) to conceive that this totally new model of a state, in which nothing escaped a change, was made with a view to its internal relations only.

In the Revolution of France two sorts of men were principally concerned in giving a character and determination to its pursuits : the philosophers and the politicians.   They took different ways, but they met in the same end.   The philosophers had one predominant object, which they pursued with a fanatical fury, that is, the utter extirpation of religion. To that every question of empire was subordinate. They had rather domineer in a parish of atheists, than rule over a Christian world.   Their temporal ambition was wholly subservient to their proselytising spirit, in which they were not exceeded by Mahomet himself.

They, who have made but superficial studies in the natural history of the human mind, have been taught to look on religious opinions as the only cause of enthusiastic zeal and sectarian propagation.   But there is no doctrine whatever, on which men can warm, that is not capable of the very same effect.   The social nature of man impels him to propagate his principles, as much as physical impulses urge him to propagate his kind.   The passions give zeal and vehemence.   The understanding bestows design and system.   The whole man moves under the discipline of his opinions.   Religion is among the most power- ful causes of enthusiasm.   When anything concerning it becomes an object of much meditation, it cannot be

indifferent to the mind. They who do not love religion, hate it. The rebels to God perfectly abhor the
author of their being. They hate Him 'with all their
heart, with all their mind, with all their soul, and with
all their strength.' He never presents Himself to their
thoughts but to menace and alarm them. They
cannot strike the sun out of heaven, but they are able
to raise a smouldering smoke that obscures Him from
their own eyes. Not being able to revenge themselves
on God, they have a delight in vicariously defacing,
degrading, torturing, and tearing in pieces, His image
in man. Let no one judge of them by what he has
conceived of them, when they were not incorporated,
and had no lead. They were then only passengers
in a common vehicle. They were then carried along
with the general motion of religion in the community,
and, without being aware of it, partook of its influence.
In that situation, at worst, their nature was left free
to counterwork their principles. They despaired of
giving any very general currency to their opinions.
They considered them as a reserved privilege for the
chosen few. But when the possibility of dominion,
lead, and propagation, presented itself, and that the
ambition, which before had so often made them hypocrites, might rather gain than lose by a daring avowal
of their sentiments, then the nature of this infernal
spirit, which has 'evil for its good,' appeared in its
full perfection. Nothing indeed but the possession

of some power can with any certainty discover what at the bottom is the true character of any man. Without reading the speeches of Vergniaux, Françias of Nantz, Isnard, and some others of that sort, it would not be easy to conceive the passion, rancour, and malice of their tongues and hearts. They worked themselves up to a perfect phrensy against religion and all its professors. They tore the reputation of the clergy to pieces by their infuriated declamations and invectives, before they lacerated their bodies by their massacres. This fanatical atheism left out, we omit the principal feature in the French Revolution, and a principal consideration with regard to the effects to be expected from a peace with it.

The other sort of men were the politicians. To them, who had little or not at all reflected on the subject, religion was in itself no object of love or hatred. They disbelieved it, and that was all. Neutral with regard to that object, they took the side which in the present state of things might best answer their purposes. They soon found that they could not do without the philosophers; and the philosophers soon made them sensible that the destruction of religion was to supply them with means of conquest first at home, and then abroad. The philosophers were the active internal agitators, and supplied the spirit and principles: the second gave the practical direction. Sometimes the one predominated in the composition, sometimes the other. The only difference between them was in the necessity of concealing the general design for a time, and in their dealing with foreign nations ; the fanatics going straight forward and openly, the politicians by the surer mode of zigzag. In the course of events this, among other causes, produced fierce and bloody contentions between them. But at the bottom they thoroughly agreed in all the objects of ambition and irreligion, and substantially in all the means of promoting these ends.

Without question, to bring about the unexampled event of the French Revolution, the concurrence of a very great number of views and passions was necessary. In that stupendous work, no one principle, by which the human mind may have its faculties at once invigorated and depraved, was left unemployed ; but I can speak it to a certainty, and support it by undoubted proofs, that the ruling principle of those who acted in the Revolution as *statesmen*, had the exterior aggrandisement of France as their ultimate end in the most minute part of the internal changes that were made. We, who of late years have been drawn from an attention to foreign affairs by the importance of our domestic discussions, cannot easily form a conception of the general eagerness of the active and energetic part of the French nation, itself the most active and energetic of all nations, previous to its

Revolution, upon that subject.   I am convinced that the foreign speculators in France, under the old government, were twenty to one of the same description then or now in England ; and few of that description there were, who did not emulously set forward the Revolution.   The whole official system, particularly in the diplomatic part, the regulars, the irregulars, down to the clerks in office, (a corps, without comparison, more numerous than the same amongst us,) co-operated in it.   All the intriguers in foreign politics, all the spies, all the intelligencers, actually or late in function, all the candidates for that sort of employment, acted solely upon that principle.

On that system of aggrandisement there was but one mind : but two violent factions arose about the means.   The first wished France, diverted from the politics of the continent, to attend solely to her marine, to feed it by an increase of commerce, and thereby to overpower England on her own element. They contended, that if England were disabled, the powers on the continent would fall into their proper subordination ; that it was England which deranged the whole continental system of Europe.   The others, who were by far the more numerous, though not the most outwardly prevalent at court, considered this plan for France as contrary to her genius, her situation, and her natural means.   They agree as to the ultimate object, the reduction of the British power, and, if possible, its naval power; but they considered an ascendency on the continent as a necessary preliminary to that undertaking. They argued, that the proceedings of England herself had proved the soundness of this policy. That her greatest and ablest statesmen had not considered the support of a continental balance against France as a deviation from the principle of her naval power, but as one of the most effectual modes of carrying it into effect. That such had been her policy ever since the Revolution, during which period the naval strength of Great Britain had gone on increasing in the direct ratio of her interference in the politics of the continent. With much stronger reason ought the politics of France to take the same direction; as well for pursuing objects which her situation would dictate to her, though England had no existence, as for counteracting the politics of that nation; to France continental politics are primary; they looked on them only of secondary consideration to England, and, however necessary, but as means necessary to an end.

What is truly astonishing, the partisans of those two opposite systems were at once prevalent, and at once employed, and in the very same transactions—the one ostensibly, the other secretly, during the latter part of the reign of Louis XV. Nor was there one court in which an ambassador resided on the part of the ministers, in which another, as a spy on him, did not also reside on the part of the king.   They who pursued the scheme for keeping peace on the continent, and particularly with Austria, acting officially and publicly, the other faction counteracting and opposing them.   These private agents were continually going from their function to the Bastile, and from the Bastile to employment, and favour again.   An inextricable cabal was formed, some of persons of rank, others of subordinates.   But by this means the corps of politicians was augmented in number, and the whole formed a body of active, adventuring, ambitious, discontented people, despising the regular ministry, despising the courts at which they were employed, despising the court which employed them

The unfortunate Louis the Sixteenth was not the first cause of the evil by which he suffered.   He came to it, as to a sort of inheritance, by the false politics of his immediate predecessor.   This system of dark and perplexed intrigue had come to its perfection before he came to the throne : and even then the Revolution stongly operated in all its causes.

There was no point on which the discontented diplomatic politicians so bitterly arraigned their cabinet, as for the decay of French influence in all others.   From quarrelling with the court, they began to complain of monarchy itself, as a system of government too variable for any regular plan of national aggrandisement. They observed, that in that sort of regimen too much depended on the personal character of the prince ; that the vicissitudes produced by the succession of princes of a different character, and even the vicissitudes produced in the same man, by the different views and inclinations belonging to youth, manhood, and age, disturbed and distracted the policy of a country made by nature for extensive empire, or, what was still more to their taste, for that sort of general over-ruling influence which prepared empire or supplied the place of it. They had continually in their hands the observations of *Machiavel* on *Livy*. They had *Montesquieu's Grandeur et Décadence des Romains* as a manual ; and they compared, with mortification, the systematic proceedings of a Roman senate with the fluctuations of a monarchy. They observed the very small additions of territory which all the power of France, actuated by all the ambition of France, had acquired in two centuries. The Romans had frequently acquired more in a single year. They severely and in every part of it criticised the reign of Louis XIV., whose irregular and desultory ambition had more provoked than endangered Europe. Indeed, they who will be at the pains of seriously considering the history of that period will see that those French politicians had some reason. They who will not take the trouble of reviewing it through all its wars and all its negotiations,

I

will consult the short but judicious criticism of the Marquis de Montalembert on that subject. It may be read separately from his ingenious system of fortification and military defence, on the practical merit of which I am unable to form a judgment.

The diplomatic politicians of whom I speak, and who formed by far the majority in that class, made disadvantageous comparisons even between their more legal and formalising monarchy, and the monarchies of other states, as a system of power and influence. They observed that France not only lost ground herself, but, through the languor and unsteadiness of her pursuits, and from her aiming through commerce at naval force which she never could attain without losing more on one side than she could gain on the other, that three great powers, each of them (as military states) capable of balancing her, had grown up on the continent. Russia and Prussia had been created almost within memory; and Austria, though not a new power, and even curtailed in territory, was, by the very collision in which she lost that territory, greatly improved in her military discipline and force. During the reign of Maria Theresa the interior economy of the country was made more to correspond with the support of great armies than formerly it had been. As to Prussia, a merely military power, they observed that one war had enriched her with as considerable a conquest as

France had acquired in centuries. Russia had broken the Turkish power by which Austria might be, as formerly she had been, balanced in favour of France. They felt it with pain, that the two northern powers of Sweden and Denmark were in general under the sway of Russia ; or that, at best, France kept up a very doubtful conflict, with many fluctuations of fortune, and at an enormous expense, in Sweden. In Holland, the French party seemed, if not extinguished, at least utterly obscured, and kept under by a stadtholder, leaning for support sometimes on Great Britain, sometimes on Prussia, sometimes on both, never on France. Even the spreading of the Bourbon family had become merely a family accommodation ; and had little effect on the national politics. This alliance, they said, extinguished Spain by destroying all its energy, without adding anything to the real power of France in the accession of the forces of its great rival. In Italy, the same family accommodation, the same national insignificance, were equally visible. What cure for the radical weakness of the French monarchy, to which all the means which wit could devise, or nature and fortune could bestow, towards universal empire, was not of force to give life, or vigour, or consistency,— but in a Republic? Out the word came ; and it never went back.

Whether they reasoned right or wrong, or that

there was some mixture of right and wrong in their reasoning, I am sure, that in this manner they felt and reasoned. The different effects of a great military and ambitious republic, and of a monarchy of the same description, were constantly in their mouths. The principle was ready to operate when opportunities should offer, which few of them indeed foresaw in the extent in which they were afterwards presented; but these opportunities, in some degree or other, they all ardently wished for.

When I was in Paris in 1773, the treaty of 1756 between Austria and France was deplored as a national calamity; because it united France in friendship with a power at whose expense alone they could hope any continental aggrandisement. When the first partition of Poland was made, in which France had no share, and which had further aggrandised every one of the three powers of which they were most jealous, I found them in a perfect phrensy of rage and indignation : not that they were hurt at the shocking and uncoloured violence and injustice of that partition, but at the debility, improvidence, and want of activity, in their government, in not preventing it as a means of aggrandisement to their rivals, or in not contriving, by exchanges of some kind or other, to obtain their share of advantage from that robbery.

In that or nearly in that state of things and of opinions, came the Austrian match; which promised to draw the knot, as afterwards in effect it did, still more closely between the old rival houses. This added exceedingly to their hatred and contempt of their monarchy. It was for this reason that the late glorious queen, who on all accounts was formed to produce general love and admiration, and whose life was as mild and beneficent as her death was beyond example great and heroic, became so very soon and so very much the object of an implacable rancour, never to be extinguished but in her blood. When I wrote my letter in answer to M. de Menonville, in the beginning of January, 1791, I had good reason for thinking that this description of revolutionists did not so early nor so steadily point their murderous designs at the martyr king as at the royal heroine. It was accident, and the momentary depression of that part of the faction, that gave to the husband the happy priority in death.

From this their restless desire of an over-ruling influence, they bent a very great part of their designs and efforts to revive the old French party, which was a democratic party in Holland, and to make a revolution there. They were happy at the troubles which the singular imprudence of Joseph the Second had stirred up in the Austrian Netherlands. They rejoiced when they saw him irritate his subjects, profess philosophy, send away the Dutch garrisons, and dismantle his fortifications. As to Holland, they never forgave either the king or the ministry, for suffering that object, which 'they justly looked on as principal in their design of reducing the power of England, to escape out of their hands. This was the true secret of the commercial treaty, made, on their part, against all the old rules and principles of commerce, with a view of diverting the English nation, by a pursuit of immediate profit, from an attention to the progress of France in its designs upon that republic. The system of the economists, which led to the general opening of commerce, facilitated that treaty, but did not produce it. They were in despair when they found that by the vigour of Mr. Pitt, supported in this point by Mr. Fox and the opposition, the object to which they had sacrificed their manufactures was lost to their ambition.

This eager desire of raising France from the condition into which she had fallen, as they conceived, from her monarchical imbecility, had been the mainspring of their precedent interference in that unhappy American quarrel, the bad effects of which to this nation have not, as yet, fully disclosed themselves. These sentiments had been long lurking in their breasts, though their views were only discovered now and then, in heat and as by escapes; but on this occasion they exploded suddenly. They were professed with ostentation and propagated with zeal. These sentiments were not produced, as some think,

by their American alliance.   The American alliance
was produced by their republican principles and republican policy.   This new relation undoubtedly did much.
The discourses and cabals that it produced, the
intercourse that it established, and, above all, the
example, which made it seem practicable to establish
a republic in a great extent of country, finished the
work, and gave to that part of the revolutionary
faction a degree of strength which required other
energies than the late king possessed, to resist, or
even to restrain.   It spread everywhere ; but it was
nowhere more prevalent than in the heart of the
court.   The palace of Versailles, by its language,
seemed a forum of democracy.   To have pointed out
to most of those politicians, from their dispositions and
movements, what has since happened, the fall of their
own monarchy, of their own laws, of their own religion,
would have been to furnish a motive the more for
pushing forward a system on which they considered all
these things as encumbrances.   Such in truth they
were.   And we have seen them succeed not only in
the destruction of their monarchy, but in all the objects
of ambition that they proposed from that destruction.

When I contemplate the scheme on which France
is formed, and when I compare it with these systems,
with which it is, and ever must be, in conflict, those
things which seem as defects in her polity are the
very things which make me tremble.   The states of

the Christian world have grown up to their present magnitude in a great length of time, and by a great variety of accidents. They have been improved to what we see them with greater or less degrees of felicity and skill. Not one of them has been formed upon a regular plan or with any unity of design. As their constitutions are not systematical, they have not been directed to any *peculiar* end, eminently distinguished, and superseding every other. The objects which they embrace are of the greatest possible variety, and have become in a manner infinite. In all these old countries the state has been made to the people, and not the people conformed to the state. Every state has pursued not only every sort of social advantage, but it has cultivated the welfare of every individual. His wants, his wishes, even his tastes, have been consulted. This comprehensive scheme virtually produced a degree of personal liberty in forms the most adverse to it. That liberty was found, under monarchies styled absolute, in a degree unknown to the ancient commonwealths. From hence the powers of all our modern states meet, in all their movements, with some obstruction. It is therefore no wonder, that, when these states are to be considered as machines to operate for some one great end, this dissipated and balanced force is not easily concentred, or made to bear with the whole force of the nation upon one point.

The British state is, without question, that which pursues the greatest variety of ends, and is the least disposed to sacrifice any one of them to another, or to the whole. It aims at taking in the entire circle of human desires, and securing for them their fair enjoyment. Our legislature has been ever closely connected, in its most efficient part, with individual feeling, and individual interest. Personal liberty, the most lively of these feelings and the most important of these interests, which in other European countries has rather arisen from the system of manners and the habitudes of life than from the laws of the state, (in which it flourished more from neglect than attention,) in England has been a direct object of government.

On this principle England would be the weakest power in the whole system. Fortunately, however, the great riches of this kingdom, arising from a variety of causes, and the disposition of the people, which is as great to spend as to accumulate, has easily afforded a disposable surplus that gives a mighty momentum to the state. This difficulty, with these advantages to overcome it, has called forth the talents of the English financiers, who, by the surplus of industry poured out by prodigality, have outdone everything which has been accomplished in other nations. The present minister has outdone his predecessors; and, as a minister of revenue, is far above my power of praise. But still there are cases in which England feels more than several others (though they all feel) the perplexity of an immense body of balanced advantages, and of individual demands, and of some irregularity in the whole mass.

France differs essentially from all those governments, which are formed without system, which exist by habit, and which are confused with the multitude, and with the complexity of their pursuits. What now stands as government in France is struck out at a heat. The design is wicked, immoral, impious, oppressive; but it is spirited and daring; it is systematic; it is simple in its principle; it has unity and consistency in perfection. In that country entirely to cut off a branch of commerce, to extinguish a manufacture, to destroy the circulation of money, to violate credit, to suspend the course of agriculture, even to burn a city, or to lay waste a province of their own, does not cost them a moment's anxiety. To them the will, the wish, the want, the liberty, the toil, the blood of individuals, is as nothing. Individuality is left out of their scheme of government. The state is all in all. Everything is referred to the production of force; afterwards, everything is trusted to the use of it. It is military in its principle, in its maxims, in its spirit, and in all its movements. The state has dominion and conquest for its sole objects; dominion over minds by proselytism, over bodies by arms.

Thus constituted, with an immense body of natural

means which are lessened in their amount only to be increased in their effect, France has, since the accomplishment of the Revolution, a complete unity in its direction. It has destroyed every resource of the state which depends upon opinion and the good-will of individuals. The riches of convention disappear. The advantages of nature in some measure remain : even these, I admit, are astonishingly lessened ; the command over what remains is complete and absolute. We go about asking when assignats will expire, and we laugh at the last price of them. But what signifies the fate of those tickets of despotism? The despotism will find despotic means of supply. They have found the short cut to the productions of nature, while others, in pursuit of them, are obliged to wind through the labyrinth of a very intricate state of society. They seize upon the fruit of the labour ; they seize upon the labourer himself. Were France but half of what it is in population, in compactness, in applicability of its force, situated as it is, and being what it is, it would be too strong for most of the states of Europe, constituted as they are, and proceeding as they proceed. Would it be wise to estimate what the world of Europe, as well as the world of Asia, had to dread from Genghiz Khân, upon a contemplation of the resources of the cold and barren spot in the remotest Tartary, from whence first issued that scourge of the human race ? Ought we to judge from the excise and stamp duties of the rocks, or from the paper circulation of the sands of Arabia, the power by which Mahomet and his tribes laid hold at once on the two most powerful empires of the world ; beat one of them totally to the ground, broke to pieces the other, and, in not much longer space of time than I have lived, overturned govern- ments, laws, manners, religion, and extended an empire from the Indus to the Pyrenees ?

Material resources never have supplied, nor ever can supply, the want of unity in design, and constancy in pursuit. But unity in design, and perseverance and boldness in pursuit, have never wanted resources, and never will. We have not considered as we ought the dreadful energy of a state in which the property has nothing to do with the government. Reflect, my dear Sir, reflect again and again, on a government, in which the property is in complete subjection, and where nothing rules but the mind of desperate men. The condition of a commonwealth not governed by its property was a combination of things which the learned and ingenious speculator Harrington, who has tossed about society into all forms, never could imagine to be possible. We have seen it ; the world has felt it ; and if the world will shut their eyes to this state of things, they will feel it more. The rulers there have found their resources in crimes. The discovery is dreadful ; the mine exhaustless.

They have everything to gain, and they have nothing to lose. They have a boundless inheritance in hope ; and there is no medium for them, betwixt the highest elevation, and death with infamy. Never can they, who, from the miserable servitude of the desk, have been raised to empire, again submit to the bondage of a starving bureau, or the profit of copying music, or writing plaidoyers by the sheet. It has made me often smile in bitterness, when I have heard talk of an indemnity to such men, provided they return to their allegiance.

From all this, what is my inference ? It is, that this new system of robbery in France cannot be rendered safe by any art ; that it *must* be destroyed, or that it will destroy all Europe ; that to destroy that enemy, by some means or other, the force opposed to it should be made to bear some analogy and resemblance to the force and spirit which that system exerts ; that war ought to be made against it, in its vulnerable parts. These are my inferences. In one word, with this republic nothing independent can co-exist. The errors of Louis XVI. were more pardonable to prudence, than any of those of the same kind into which the allied courts may fall. They have the benefit of his dreadful example.

The unhappy Louis XVI. was a man of the best intentions that probably ever reigned. He was by no means deficient in talents. He had a most laudable desire to supply by general reading, and even by the acquisition of elemental knowledge, an education in all points originally defective ; but nobody told him, (and it was no wonder he should not himself divine it,) that the world of which he read, and the world in which he lived, were no longer the same. Desirous of doing everything for the best, fearful of cabal, distrusting his own judgment, he sought his ministers of all kinds upon public testimony. But as courts are the field for caballers, the public is the theatre for mountebanks and impostors. The cure for both those evils is in the discernment of the prince. But an accurate and penetrating discernment is what in a young prince could not be looked for.

His conduct in its principle was not unwise ; but, like most other of his well-meant designs, it failed in his hands. It failed partly from mere ill-fortune, to which speculators are rarely pleased to assign that very large share to which she is justly entitled in all human affairs. The failure, perhaps, in part was owing to his suffering his system to be vitiated and disturbed by those intrigues, which it is, humanly speaking, impossible wholly to prevent in courts, or indeed under any form of government. However, with these aberrations, he gave himself over to a succession of the statesmen of public opinion. In other things he thought that he might be a king on the terms of his predecessors. He was conscious of the purity of his heart and the general good tendency of his government. He flattered himself, as most men in his situation will, that he might consult his ease without danger to his safety. It is not at all wonderful that both he and his ministers, giving way abundantly in other respects to innovation, should take up in policy with the tradition of their monarchy. Under his ancestors the monarchy had subsisted, and even been strengthened, by the generation or support of republics. First, the Swiss republics grew under the guardianship of the French monarchy. The Dutch republics were hatched and cherished under the same incubation. Afterwards, a republican constitution was, under the influence of France, established in the empire against the pretensions of its chief. Even whilst the monarchy of France, by a series of wars and negotiations, and lastly by the treaties of Westphalia, had obtained the establishment of the Protestants in Germany as a law of the empire, the same monarchy under Louis XIII. had force enough to destroy the republican system of the Protestants at home.

Louis XVI. was a diligent reader of history. But the very lamp of prudence blinded him. The guide of human life led him astray. A silent revolution in the moral world preceded the political, and prepared it. It became of more importance than ever what

examples were given, and what measures were adopted.
Their causes no longer lurked in the recesses of
cabinets, or in the private conspiracies of the factious.
They were no longer to be controlled by the force
and influence of the grandees, who formerly had been
able to stir up troubles by their discontents, and to
quiet them by their corruption. The chain of
subordination, even in cabal and sedition, was broken
in its most important links. It was no longer the
great and the populace. Other interests were formed,
other dependencies, other connexions, other communi-
cations. The middle classes had swelled far beyond
their former proportion. Like whatever is the most
effectively rich and great in society, these classes
became the seat of all the active politics; and the
preponderating weight to decide on them. There
were all the energies by which fortune is acquired:
there the consequence of their success. There were
all the talents which assert their pretensions, and are
impatient of the place which settled society prescribes
to them. These descriptions had got between the
great and the populace; and the influence on the
lower classes was with them. The spirit of ambition
had taken possession of this class as violently as ever
it had done of any other. They felt the importance
of this situation. The correspondence of the monied
and the mercantile world, the literary intercourse of
academies, but, above all, the press, of which they

had in a manner entire possession, made a kind of electric communication everywhere. The press in reality has made every government, in its spirit, almost democratic. Without it the great, the first movements in this Revolution could not, perhaps, have been given. But the spirit of ambition, now for the first time connected with the spirit of speculation, was not to be restrained at will. There was no longer any means of arresting a principle in its course. When Louis XVI., under the influence of the enemies to monarchy, meant to found but one republic, he set up two. When he meant to take away half the crown of his neighbour, he lost the whole of his own. Louis XVI. could not with impunity countenance a new republic : yet between his throne and that dangerous lodgment for an enemy, which he had erected, he had the whole Atlantic for a ditch. He had for an out-work the English nation itself, friendly to liberty, adverse to that mode of it. He was surrounded by a rampart of monarchies, most of them allied to him, and generally under his influence. Yet even thus secured, a republic erected under his auspices, and dependent on his power, became fatal to his throne. The very money which he had lent to support this republic, by a good faith, which to him operated as perfidy, was punctually paid to his enemies, and became a resource in the hands of his assassins.

K

With this example before their eyes, do any ministers in England, do any ministers in Austria, really flatter themselves that they can erect, not on the remote shores of the Atlantic, but in their view, in their vicinity, in absolute contact with one of them, not a commercial but a martial republic—a republic not of simple husbandmen or fishermen, but of intriguers, and of warriors—a republic of a character the most restless, the most enterprising, the most impious, the most fierce and bloody, the most hypocritical and perfidious, the most bold and daring, that ever has been seen, or indeed that can be conceived to exist, without bringing on their own certain ruin ?

Such is the republic to which we are going to give a place in civilised fellowship : the republic, which, with joint consent, we are going to establish in the centre of Europe, in a post that overlooks and commands every other state, and which eminently confronts and menaces this kingdom.

You cannot fail to observe that I speak as if the allied powers were actually consenting, and not compelled by events to the establishment of this faction in France. The words have not escaped me. You will hereafter naturally expect that I should make them good. But whether in adopting this measure we are madly active, or weakly passive, or pusillanimously panic struck, the effects will be the same. You may call this faction, which has eradicated the monarchy,—expelled the proprietary, persecuted religion, and trampled upon law,—you may call this France if you please : but of the ancient France nothing remains but its central geography ; its iron frontier; its spirit of ambition; its audacity of enterprise ; its perplexing intrigue.   These, and these alone, remain : and they remain heightened in their principle and augmented in their means.   All the former correctives, whether of virtue or of weakness, which existed in the old monarchy, are gone.   No single new corrective is to be found in the whole body of the new institutions.   How should such a thing be found there, when everything has been chosen with care and selection to forward all those ambitious designs and dispositions, not to control them ?   The whole is a body of ways and means for the supply of dominion, without one heterogeneous particle in it.

Here I suffer you to breathe, and leave to your meditation what has occurred to me on the *genius and character* of the French Revolution.   From having this before us, we may be better able to determine on the first question I proposed, that is, how far nations, called foreign, are likely to be affected with the system established within that territory.   I intended to proceed next on the question of her facilities, from *the internal state of other nations, and particularly of this*, for obtaining her ends : but I ought to be aware that my notions are controverted.—I mean, therefore, in my next letter, to take notice of what, in that way, has been recommended to me as the most deserving of notice. In the examination of those pieces, I shall have occasion to discuss some others of the topics to which I have called your attention. You know that the letters which I now send to the press, as well as a part of what is to follow, have been in their substance long since written. A circumstance which your partiality alone could make of importance to you, but which to the public is of no importance at all, retarded their appearance. The late events which press upon us obliged me to make some additions; but no substantial change in the matter.

This discussion, my friend, will be long. But the matter is serious; and if ever the fate of the world could be truly said to depend on a particular measure, it is upon this peace. For the present, farewell.

V.—'PETER PLYMLEY'S LETTERS'

BY SYDNEY SMITH

(LETTERS II., VI., VII., IX.)

(*The pamphleteering spirit is strong in almost
all Sydney Smith's 'Contributions to the* Edinburgh
Review,' *but the form and subjects of those contributions
exclude them here. Of his two great pamphlet issues
proper,* Peter Plymley's Letters *and those* To Archdeacon Singleton, *the former are, though perhaps of
less polished and perfect wit than the latter, more
distinctly political, and have more of that* diable au
corps *which Voltaire considered necessary to success in
the arts. They have also the advantage that, while
the* Letters to Archdeacon Singleton, *though not an
avowed recantation, are in the nature of a palinode—
always an awkward thing—*Plymley *is frankly and
confidently, not to say wantonly, aggressive. These*
Letters, *ten in number, were written just after the
fall of the mainly Whig Ministry of 'All the Talents,'
to which Sydney had been indebted for his prefer-*

ment of Foston, and which lost its position not least owing to its intended support of the ' Catholic' claims. Those claims were not admitted for twenty years later; and Sydney's advocacy of them was regarded as a little too exuberant by some even of his own party. But there is no doubt that the Letters *had a great influence in laughing if not in arguing sections of the public round to the Emancipation side.)*

LETTER II

DEAR ABRAHAM—The Catholic not respect an oath ! why not ? What upon earth has kept him out of Parliament, or excluded him from all the offices whence he is excluded, but his respect for oaths ? There is no law which prohibits a Catholic to sit in Parliament. There could be no such law; because it is impossible to find out what passes in the interior of any man's mind. Suppose it were in contemplation to exclude all men from certain offices who contended for the legality of taking tithes : the only mode of discovering that fervid love of decimation which I know you to possess would be to tender you an oath " against that damnable doctrine, that it is lawful for a spiritual man to take, abstract, appropriate, subduct, or lead away the tenth calf, sheep, lamb, ox, pigeon, duck," etc., etc., etc., and every other animal that ever existed, which of course the lawyers would take care to enumerate.   Now this oath I am sure you would rather die than take ; and so the Catholic is excluded from Parliament because he will not swear that he disbelieves the leading doctrines of his religion !   The Catholic asks you to abolish some oaths which oppress him ; your answer is that he does not respect oaths.   Then why subject him to the test of oaths ?   The oaths keep him out of Parliament ; why, then, he respects them.   Turn which way you will, either your laws are nugatory, or the Catholic is bound by religious obligations as you are ; but no eel in the well-sanded fist of a cook-maid, upon the eve of being skinned, ever twisted and writhed as an orthodox parson does when he is compelled by the gripe of reason to admit anything in favour of a dissenter.

I will not dispute with you whether the Pope be or be not the Scarlet Lady of Babylon.   I hope it is not so ; because I am afraid it will induce His Majesty's Chancellor of the Exchequer to introduce several severe bills against popery, if that is the case ; and though he will have the decency to appoint a previous committee of inquiry as to the fact, the committee will be garbled, and the report inflammatory.   Leaving this to be settled as he pleases to settle it, I wish to inform you, that, previously to the bill last passed in favour of the Catholics, at the suggestion of Mr. Pitt, and for his satisfaction, the opinions of six of the most celebrated of the foreign Catholic universities were taken as to the right of the Pope to interfere in the temporal concerns of any country. The answer cannot possibly leave the shadow of a doubt, even in the mind of Baron Maseres; and Dr. Rennel would be compelled to admit it, if three Bishops lay dead at the very moment the question were put to him. To this answer might be added also the solemn declaration and signature of all the Catholics in Great Britain.

I should perfectly agree with you, if the Catholics admitted such a dangerous dispensing power in the hands of the Pope; but they all deny it, and laugh at it, and are ready to abjure it in the most decided manner you can devise. They obey the Pope as the spiritual head of their Church; but are you really so foolish as to be imposed upon by mere names? What matters it the seven-thousandth part of a farthing who is the spiritual head of any Church? Is not Mr. Wilberforce at the head of the Church of Clapham? Is not Dr. Letsom at the head of the Quaker Church? Is not the General Assembly at the head of the Church of Scotland? How is the government disturbed by these many-headed Churches? or in what way is the power of the Crown augmented by this almost nominal dignity?

The King appoints a fast-day once a year, and he makes the bishops: and if the government would take half the pains to keep the Catholics out of the arms of France that it does to widen Temple Bar, or improve

Snow Hill, the King would get into his hands the appointments of the titular Bishops of Ireland. Both Mr. C——'s sisters enjoy pensions more than sufficient to place the two greatest dignitaries of the Irish Catholic Church entirely at the disposal of the Crown. Everybody who knows Ireland knows perfectly well, that nothing would be easier, with the expenditure of a little money, than to preserve enough of the ostensible appointment in the hands of the Pope to satisfy the scruples of the Catholics, while the real nomination remained with the Crown. But, as I have before said, the moment the very name of Ireland is mentioned, the English seem to bid adieu to common feeling, common prudence, and common sense, and to act with the barbarity of tyrants and the fatuity of idiots.

Whatever your opinion may be of the follies of the Roman Catholic religion, remember they are the follies of four millions of human beings, increasing rapidly in numbers, wealth, and intelligence, who, if firmly united with this country, would set at defiance the power of France, and if once wrested from their alliance with England, would in three years render its existence as an independent nation absolutely impossible. You speak of danger to the Establishment: I request to know when the Establishment was ever so much in danger as when Hoche was in Bantry Bay, and whether all the books of Bossuet, or the arts of the Jesuits, were half so terrible? Mr. Perceval and his parsons forget all this, in their horror lest twelve or fourteen old women may be converted to holy water and Catholic nonsense. They never see that, while they are saving these venerable ladies from perdition, Ireland may be lost, England broken down, and the Protestant Church, with all its deans, prebendaries, Percevals, and Kennels, be swept into the vortex of oblivion.

Do not, I beseech you, ever mention to me again the name of Dr. Duigenan. I have been in every corner of Ireland, and have studied its present strength and condition with no common labour. Be assured Ireland does not contain at this moment less than five millions of people. There were returned in the year 1791 to the hearth tax 701,000 houses, and there is no kind of question that there were about 50,000 houses omitted in that return. Taking, however, only the number returned for the tax, and allowing the average of six to a house (a very small average for a potato-fed people), this brings the population to 4,200,000 people in the year 1791 : and it can be shown from the clearest evidence (and Mr. Newenham in his book shows it), that Ireland for the last fifty years has increased in its population at the rate of 50 or 60,000 per annum; which leaves the present population of Ireland at about five millions, after every possible deduction for *existing circumstances, just and necessary wars, monstrous and unnatural rebellions,* and all other sources of human destruction. Of this population, two out of ten are Protestants; and the half of the Protestant population are Dissenters, and as inimical to the Church as the Catholics themselves. In this state of things thumbscrews and whipping—admirable engines of policy as they must be considered to be—will not ultimately avail. The Catholics will hang over you; they will watch for the moment, and compel you hereafter to give them ten times as much, against your will, as they would now be contented with, if it were voluntarily surrendered. Remember what happened in the American war, when Ireland compelled you to give her everything she asked, and to renounce, in the most explicit manner, your claim of Sovereignty over her. God Almighty grant the folly of these present men may not bring on such another crisis of public affairs!

What are your dangers which threaten the Establishment?—Reduce this declamation to a point, and let us understand what you mean. The most ample allowance does not calculate that there would be more than twenty members who were Roman Catholics in one house, and ten in the other, if the Catholic emancipation were carried into effect. Do you mean that these thirty members would bring in a bill to take away the tithes from the Protestant, and to pay them to the Catholic clergy? Do you mean that a Catholic

general would march his army into the House of Commons, and purge it of Mr. Perceval and Dr. Duigenan?
or, that the theological writers would become all of
a sudden more acute or more learned, if the present
civil incapacities were removed? Do you fear for
your tithes, or your doctrines, or your person, or the
English Constitution? Every fear, taken separately,
is so glaringly absurd, that no man has the folly or
the boldness to state it. Every one conceals his
ignorance, or his baseness, in a stupid general panic,
which, when called on, he is utterly incapable of
explaining. Whatever you think of the Catholics,
there they are—you cannot get rid of them; your
alternative is to give them a lawful place for stating
their grievances, or an unlawful one: if you do not
admit them to the House of Commons, they will hold
their parliament in Potatoe Place, Dublin, and be ten
times as violent and inflammatory as they would be in
Westminster. Nothing would give me such an idea
of security as to see twenty or thirty Catholic gentlemen in Parliament, looked upon by all the Catholics
as the fair and proper organ of their party. I should
have thought it the height of good fortune that such
a wish existed on their part, and the very essence of
madness and ignorance to reject it. Can you murder
the Catholics? Can you neglect them? They are
too numerous for both these expedients. What remains to be done is obvious to every human being—

but to that man who, instead of being a Methodist
preacher, is, for the curse of us and our children, and
for the ruin of Troy and the misery of good old Priam
and his sons, become a legislator and a politician.

A distinction, I perceive, is taken by one of the
most feeble noblemen in Great Britain, between persecution and the deprivation of political power; whereas,
there is no more distinction between these two things
than there is between him who makes the distinction
and a booby. If I strip off the relic-covered jacket
of a Catholic, and give him twenty stripes . . . I persecute; if I say, Everybody in the town where you
live shall be a candidate for lucrative and honourable
offices, but you, who are a Catholic . . . I do not
persecute! What barbarous nonsense is this! as if
degradation was not as great an evil as bodily pain or
as severe poverty: as if I could not be as great a
tyrant by saying, You shall not enjoy—as by saying,
You shall suffer. The English, I believe, are as
truly religious as any nation in Europe: I know no
greater blessing; but it carries with it this evil in its
train, that any villain who will bawl out, ' *The Church
is in danger!*' may get a place and a good pension;
and that any administration who will do the same
thing may bring a set of men into power who, at a
moment of stationary and passive piety, would be
hooted by the very boys in the streets. But it is not
all religion; it is, in great part, the narrow and ex-

clusive spirit which delights to keep the common blessings of sun and air and freedom from other human beings. 'Your religion has always been degraded ; you are in the dust, and I will take care you never rise again. I should enjoy less the possession of an earthly good by every additional person to whom it was extended.' You may not be aware of it yourself, most reverend Abraham, but you deny their freedom to the Catholics upon the same principle that Sarah your wife refuses to give the receipt for a ham or a gooseberry dumpling : she values her receipts, not because they secure to her a certain flavour, but because they remind her that her neighbours want it :—a feeling laughable in a priestess, shameful in a priest ; venial when it withholds the blessings of a ham, tyrannical and execrable when it narrows the boon of religious freedom.

You spend a great deal of ink about the character of the present prime minister. Grant you all that you write—I say, I fear he will ruin Ireland, and pursue a line of policy destructive to the true interest of his country : and then you tell me, he is faithful to Mrs. Perceval, and kind to the Master Percevals ! These are, undoubtedly, the first qualifications to be looked to in a time of the most serious public danger ; but somehow or another (if public and private virtues must always be incompatible), I should prefer that he destroyed the domestic happiness of Wood or Cockell, owed for the veal of the preceding year, whipped his boys, and saved his country.

The late administration did not do right ; they did not build their measures upon the solid basis of facts. They should have caused several Catholics to have been dissected after death by surgeons of either religion ; and the report to have been published with accompanying plates. If the viscera, and other organs of life, had been found to be the same as in Protestant bodies ; if the provisions of nerves, arteries, cerebrum, and cerebellum, had been the same as we are provided with, or as the Dissenters are now known to possess ; then, indeed, they might have met Mr. Perceval upon a proud eminence, and convinced the country at large of the strong probability that the Catholics are really human creatures, endowed with the feelings of men, and entitled to all their rights. But instead of this wise and prudent measure, Lord Howick, with his usual precipitation, brings forward a bill in their favour, without offering the slightest proof to the country that they were anything more than horses and oxen. The person who shows the lama at the corner of Piccadilly has the precaution to write up—*Allowed by Sir Joseph Banks to be a real quadruped*, so his Lordship might have said—*Allowed by the bench of Bishops to be real human creatures.* . . . I could write you twenty letters upon this subject ; but I am tired, and so I suppose are you. Our friendship is now of forty years' standing; you know me to be a truly religious man; but I shudder to see religion treated like a cockade, or a pint of beer, and made the instrument of a party. I love the king, but I love the people as well as the king; and if I am sorry to see his old age molested, I am much more sorry to see four millions of Catholics baffled in their just expectations. If I love Lord Grenville, and Lord Howick, it is because they love their country; if I abhor . . . it is because I know there is but one man among them who is not laughing at the enormous folly and credulity of the country, and that he is an ignorant and mischievous bigot. As for the light and frivolous jester, of whom it is your misfortune to think so highly, learn, my dear Abraham, that this political Killigrew, just before the breaking-up of the last administration, was in actual treaty with them for a place; and if they had survived twenty-four hours longer, he would have been now declaiming against the cry of No Popery! instead of inflaming it. With this practical comment on the baseness of human nature, I bid you adieu!

LETTER VI

DEAR ABRAHAM—What amuses me the most is to hear of the *indulgences* which the Catholics have received, and their exorbitance in not being satisfied with those indulgences: now if you complain to me that a man is obtrusive and shameless in his requests, and that it is impossible to bring him to reason, I must first of all hear the whole of your conduct towards him; for you may have taken from him so much in the first instance that, in spite of a long series of restitution, a vast latitude for petition may still remain behind.

There is a village, no matter where, in which the inhabitants, on one day in the year, sit down to a dinner prepared at the common expense : by an extraordinary piece of tyranny, which Lord Hawkesbury would call the wisdom of the village ancestors, the inhabitants of three of the streets, about a hundred years ago, seized upon the inhabitants of the fourth street, bound them hand and foot, laid them upon their backs, and compelled them to look on while the rest were stuffing themselves with beef and beer ; the next year the inhabitants of the persecuted street, though they contributed an equal quota of the expense, were treated precisely in the same manner. The tyranny grew into a custom ; and, as the manner of our nature is, it was considered as the most sacred of all duties to keep these poor fellows without their annual dinner. The village was so tenacious of this practice, that nothing could induce them to resign it ; every enemy to it was looked upon as a disbeliever in Divine Providence, and any nefarious churchwarden who wished to succeed in his election had nothing to do but to represent his antagonist as an abolitionist. in order to frustrate his ambition, endanger his life, and throw the village into a state of the most dreadful commotion. By degrees, however, the obnoxious street grew to be so well peopled, and its inhabitants so firmly united, that their oppressors, more afraid of injustice, were more disposed to be just. At the next dinner they are unbound, the year after allowed to sit upright, then a bit of bread and a glass of water; till at last, after a long series of concessions, they are emboldened to ask, in pretty plain terms, that they may be allowed to sit down at the bottom of the table, and to fill their bellies as well as the rest. Forthwith a general cry of shame and scandal: 'Ten years ago, were you not laid upon your backs? Don't you remember what a great thing you thought it to get a piece of bread? How thankful you were for cheese parings? Have you forgotten that memorable era, when the lord of the manor interfered to obtain for you a slice of the public pudding? And now, with an audacity only equalled by your ingratitude, you have the impudence to ask for knives and forks, and to request, in terms too plain to be mistaken, that you may sit down to table with the rest, and be indulged even with beef and beer: there are not more than half a dozen dishes which we have reserved for ourselves; the rest has been thrown open to you in the utmost profusion; you have potatoes, and carrots, suet dumplings, sops in the pan, and delicious toast and water in incredible quantities. Beef, mutton, lamb, pork, and veal are ours; and if you were not the most restless and dissatisfied of human beings, you would never think of aspiring to enjoy them.'

Is not this, my dainty Abraham, the very nonsense and the very insult which is talked to and practised upon the Catholics? You are surprised that men who have tasted of partial justice should ask for perfect justice; that he who has been robbed of coat and cloak will not be contented with the restitution of one of his garments. He would be a very lazy blockhead if he were content, and I (who, though an inhabitant of the village, have preserved, thank God, some sense of justice) most earnestly counsel these half-fed claimants to persevere in their just demands, till they are admitted to a more complete share of a dinner for which they pay as much as the others; and if they see a little attenuated lawyer squabbling at the head of their opponents, let them desire him to empty his pockets, and to pull out all the pieces of duck, fowl, and pudding which he has filched from the public feast, to carry home to his wife and children.

You parade a great deal upon the vast concessions made by this country to the Irish before the Union. I deny that any voluntary concession was ever made by England to Ireland. What did Ireland ever ask that was granted? What did she ever demand that

was not refused? How did she get her Mutiny Bill—
a limited Parliament—a repeal of Poyning's Law—a
constitution? Not by the concessions of England,
but by her fears. When Ireland asked for all these
things upon her knees, her petitions were rejected
with Percevalism and contempt; when she demanded
them with the voice of 60,000 armed men, they were
granted with every mark of consternation and dismay.
Ask of Lord Auckland the fatal consequences of
trifling with such a people as the Irish. He himself
was the organ of these refusals. As secretary to the
Lord Lieutenant, the insolence and the tyranny of this
country passed through his hands. Ask him if he
remembers the consequences. Ask him if he has
forgotten that memorable evening when he came down
booted and mantled to the House of Commons,
when he told the House he was about to set off for
Ireland that night, and declared before God, if he did
not carry with him a compliance with all their demands,
Ireland was for ever lost to this country. The present
generation have forgotten this; but I have not forgotten it; and I know, hasty and undignified as the
submission of England then was, that Lord Auckland
was right, that the delay of a single day might very
probably have separated the two peoples for ever.
The terms submission and fear are galling terms
when applied from the lesser nation to the greater;
but it is the plain historical truth, it is the natural

consequence of injustice, it is the predicament in which every country places itself which leaves such a mass of hatred and discontent by its side. No empire is powerful enough to endure it ; it would exhaust the strength of China, and sink it with all its mandarins and tea-kettles to the bottom of the deep. By refusing them justice now when you are strong enough to refuse them anything more than justice, you will act over again, with the Catholics, the same scene of mean and precipitate submission which disgraced you before America, and before the volunteers of Ireland. We shall live to hear the Hampstead Protestant pronouncing such extravagant panegyrics upon holy water, and paying such fulsome compliments to the thumbs and offals of departed saints, that parties will change sentiments, and Lord Henry Petty and Sam Whitbread take a spell at No Popery. The wisdom of Mr. Fox was alike employed in teaching his country justice when Ireland was weak, and dignity when Ireland was strong. We are fast pacing round the same miserable circle of ruin and imbecility. Alas ! where is our guide ?

You say that Ireland is a millstone about our necks ; that it would be better for us if Ireland were sunk at the bottom of the sea ; that the Irish are a nation of irreclaimable savages and barbarians. How often have I heard these sentiments fall from the plump and thoughtless squire, and from the thriving

English shopkeeper, who has never felt the rod of an Orange master upon his back. Ireland a millstone about your neck ! Why is it not a stone of Ajax in your hand ? I agree with you most cordially that, governed as Ireland now is, it would be a vast accession of strength if the waves of the sea were to rise and engulf her to-morrow. At this moment, opposed as we are to all the world, the annihilation of one of the most fertile islands on the face of the globe, containing five millions of human creatures, would be one of the most solid advantages which could happen to this country. I doubt very much, in spite of all the just abuse which has been lavished upon Bonaparte, whether there is any one of his conquered countries the blotting out of which would be as beneficial to him as the destruction of Ireland would be to us : of countries I speak differing in language from the French, little habituated to their intercourse, and inflamed with all the resentments of a recently conquered people. Why will you attribute the turbulence of our people to any cause but the right—to any cause but your own scandalous oppression ? If you tie your horse up to a gate, and beat him cruelly, is he vicious because he kicks you ? If you have plagued and worried a mastiff dog for years, is he mad because he flies at you whenever he sees you ? Hatred is an active, troublesome passion. Depend upon it, whole nations have always some reason for their hatred. Before you refer the turbulence of the Irish to incurable defects in their character, tell me if you have treated them as friends and equals? Have you protected their commerce? Have you respected their religion? Have you been as anxious for their freedom as your own? Nothing of all this. What then? Why you have confiscated the territorial surface of the country twice over : you have massacred and exported her inhabitants : you have deprived fourfifths of them of every civil privilege : you have at every period made her commerce and manufactures slavishly subordinate to your own : and yet the hatred which the Irish bear to you is the result of an original turbulence of character, and of a primitive, obdurate wildness, utterly incapable of civilisation. The embroidered inanities and the sixth-form effusions of Mr. Canning are really not powerful enough to make me believe this; nor is there any authority on earth (always excepting the Dean of Christ Church) which could make it credible to me. I am sick of Mr. Canning. There is not a 'ha'porth of bread to all this sugar and sack.' I love not the cretaceous and incredible countenance of his colleague. The only opinion in which I agree with these two gentlemen is that which they entertain of each other. I am sure that the insolence of Mr. Pitt, and the unbalanced accounts of Melville, were far better than the perils of this new ignorance :—

Nonne fuit satiùs, tristes Amaryllidis iras
Atque superba pati fastidia ? nonne Menalcan ?
Quamvis ille *niger* ?

In the midst of the most profound peace, the
secret articles of the Treaty of Tilsit, in which the
destruction of Ireland is resolved upon, induce you to
rob the Danes of their fleet. After the expedition
sailed comes the Treaty of Tilsit, containing no
article, public or private, alluding to Ireland. The
state of the world, you tell me, justified us in doing
this. Just God ! do we think only of the state of the
world when there is an opportunity for robbery, for
murder, and for plunder ; and do we forget the state
of the world when we are called upon to be wise, and
good, and just ? Does the state of the world never
remind us that we have four millions of subjects
whose injuries we ought to atone for, and whose
affections we ought to conciliate ? Does the state of
the world never warn us to lay aside our infernal
bigotry, and to arm every man who acknowledges a
God, and can grasp a sword ? Did it never occur to
this administration that they might virtuously get hold
of a force ten times greater than the force of the
Danish fleet ? Was there no other way of protecting
Ireland but by bringing eternal shame upon Great
Britain, and by making the earth a den of robbers ?
See what the men whom you have supplanted would
have done. They would have rendered the invasion

of Ireland impossible, by restoring to the Catholics their long-lost rights : they would have acted in such a manner that the French would neither have wished for invasion nor dared to attempt it : they would have increased the permanent strength of the country while they preserved its reputation unsullied. Nothing of this kind your friends have done, because they are solemnly pledged to do nothing of this kind ; because, to tolerate all religions, and to equalise civil rights to all sects, is to oppose some of the worst passions of our nature—to plunder and to oppress is to gratify them all. They wanted the huzzas of mobs, and they have for ever blasted the fame of England to obtain them. Were the fleets of Holland, France, and Spain destroyed by larceny? You resisted the power of 150 sail of the line by sheer courage, and violated every principle of morals from the dread of fifteen hulks, while the expedition itself cost you three times more than the value of the larcenous matter brought away. The French trample on the laws of God and man, not for old cordage, but for kingdoms, and always take care to be well paid for their crimes. We contrive, under the present administration, to unite moral with intellectual deficiency, and to grow weaker and worse by the same action. If they had any evidence of the intended hostility of the Danes, why was it not produced? Why have the nations of Europe been allowed to feel an indignation against this country beyond the reach of all subsequent information ? Are these times, do you imagine, when we can trifle with a year of universal hatred, dally with the curses of Europe, and then regain a lost character at pleasure, by the parliamentary perspirations of the Foreign Secretary, or the solemn asseverations of the pecuniary Rose ? Believe me, Abraham, it is not under such ministers as these that the dexterity of honest Englishmen will ever equal the dexterity of French knaves; it is not in their presence that the serpent of Moses will ever swallow up the serpents of the magician.

Lord Hawkesbury says that nothing is to be granted to the Catholics from fear. What ! not even justice ? Why not ? There are four millions of disaffected people within twenty miles of your own coast. I fairly confess that the dread which I have of their physical power is with me a very strong motive for listening to their claims. To talk of not acting from fear is mere parliamentary cant. From what motive but fear, I should be glad to know, have all the improvements in our constitution proceeded ? I question if any justice has ever been done to large masses of mankind from any other motive. By what other motives can the plunderers of the Baltic suppose nations to be governed in their intercourse *with each other* ? If I say, Give this people what they ask because it is just, do you think I should get ten people to listen to me ? Would not the lesser of the two Jenkinsons be the first to treat me with contempt? The only true way to make the mass of mankind see the beauty of justice is by showing to them, in pretty plain terms, the consequences of injustice. If any body of French troops land in Ireland, the whole population of that country will rise against you to a man, and you could not possibly survive such an event three years. Such, from the bottom of my soul, do I believe to be the present state of that country; and so far does it appear to me to be impolitic and unstatesman-like to conceed anything to such a danger, that if the Catholics, in addition to their present just demands, were to petition for the perpetual removal of the said Lord Hawkesbury from his Majesty's councils, I think, whatever might be the effect upon the destinies of Europe, and however it might retard our own individual destruction, that the prayer of the petition should be instantly complied with. Canning's crocodile tears should not move me; the hoops of the maids of honour should not hide him. I would tear him from the banisters of the back stairs, and plunge him in the fishy fumes of the dirtiest of all his Cinque Ports.

LETTER VII

DEAR ABRAHAM—In the correspondence which is passing between us, you are perpetually alluding to

the Foreign Secretary; and in answer to the dangers
of Ireland, which I am pressing upon your notice, you
have nothing to urge but the confidence which you
repose in the discretion and sound sense of this
gentleman.   I can only say, that I have listened to
him long and often with the greatest attention; I
have used every exertion in my power to take a fair
measure of him, and it appears to me impossible to
hear him upon any arduous topic without perceiving
that he is eminently deficient in those solid and
serious qualities upon which, and upon which alone,
the confidence of a great country can properly repose.
He sweats and labours, and works for sense, and Mr.
Ellis seems always to think it is coming, but it does
not come; the machine can't draw up what is not to
be found in the spring; Providence has made him a
light, jesting, paragraph-writing man, and that he will
remain to his dying day.   When he is jocular he is
strong, when he is serious he is like Samson in a wig;
any ordinary person is a match for him: a song, an
ironical letter, a burlesque ode, an attack in the news-
paper upon Nicoll's eye, a smart speech of twenty
minutes, full of gross misrepresentations and clever
turns, excellent language, a spirited manner, lucky
quotation, success in provoking dull men, some half
information picked up in Pall Mall in the morning;
these are your friend's natural weapons; all these
things he can do: here I allow him to be truly great;

nay, I will be just, and go still further, if he would confine himself to these things, and consider the *facete* and the playful to be the basis of his character, he would, for that species of man, be universally regarded as a person of a very good understanding; call him a legislator, a reasoner, and the conductor of the affairs of a great nation, and it seems to me as absurd as if a butterfly were to teach bees to make honey. That he is an extraordinary writer of small poetry, and a diner out of the highest lustre, I do most readily admit. After George Selwyn, and perhaps Tickell, there has been no such man for this half-century. The Foreign Secretary is a gentleman, a respectable as well as a highly agreeable man in private life; but you may as well feed me with decayed potatoes as console me for the miseries of Ireland by the resources of his *sense* and his *discretion.* It is only the public situation which this gentleman holds which entitles me or induces me to say so much about him. He is a fly in amber, nobody cares about the fly; the only question is, How the devil did it get there? Nor do I attack him for the love of glory, but from the love of utility, as a burgomaster hunts a rat in a Dutch dyke for fear it should flood a province.

The friends of the Catholic question are, I observe, extremely embarrassed in arguing when they come to the loyalty of the Irish Catholics. As for me, I shall

go straight forward to my object, and state what I
have no manner of doubt, from an intimate knowledge
of Ireland, to be the plain truth.　Of the great Roman
Catholic proprietors, and of the Catholic prelates,
there may be a few, and but a few, who would follow
the fortunes of England at all events : there is another
set of men who, thoroughly detesting this country,
have too much property and too much character to
lose, not to wait ;for some very favourable event
before they show themselves ; but the great mass of
Catholic population, upon the slightest appearance of
a French force in that country, would rise upon you
to a man.　It is the most mistaken policy to conceal
the plain truth.　There is no loyalty among the
Catholics : they detest you as their worst oppressors,
and they will continue to detest you till you remove
the cause of their hatred.　It is in your power in six
months' time to produce a total revolution of opinions
among this people ; and in some future letter I will
show you that this is clearly the case.　At present,
see what a dreadful state Ireland is in.　The common
toast among the low Irish is, the feast of the *passover*.
Some allusion to *Bonaparte*, in a play lately acted at
Dublin, produced thunders of applause from the pit
and the galleries ; and a politician should not be
inattentive to the public feelings expressed in theatres.
Mr. Perceval thinks he has disarmed the Irish : he
has no more disarmed the Irish than he has resigned

a shilling of his own public emoluments. An Irish peasant fills the barrel of his gun full of tow dipped in oil, butters up the lock, buries it in a bog, and allows the Orange bloodhound to ransack his cottage at pleasure. Be just and kind to the Irish, and you will indeed disarm them; rescue them from the degraded servitude in which they are held by a handful of their own countrymen, and you will add four millions of brave and affectionate men to your strength. Nightly visits, Protestant inspectors, licenses to possess a pistol, or a knife and fork, the odious vigour of the *evangelical* Perceval—acts of Parliament, drawn up by some English attorney, to save you from the hatred of four millions of people—the guarding yourselves from universal disaffection by a police ; a confidence in the little cunning of Bow Street, when you might rest your security upon the eternal basis of the best feelings : this is the meanness and madness to which nations are reduced when they lose sight of the first elements of justice, without which a country can be no more secure than it can be healthy without air. I sicken at such policy and such men. The fact is, the Ministers know nothing about the present state of Ireland ; Mr. Perceval sees a few clergymen, Lord Castlereagh a few general officers, who take care, of course, to report what is pleasant rather than what is true. As for the joyous and lepid consul, he jokes upon neutral flags and frauds, jokes upon Irish rebels, jokes upon northern and western and southern foes, and gives himself no trouble upon any subject; nor is the mediocrity of the idolatrous deputy of the slightest use. Dissolved in grins, he reads no memorials upon the state of Ireland, listens to no reports, asks no questions, and is the

"*Bourn* from whom no traveller returns."

The danger of an immediate insurrection is now, I *believe*, blown over. You have so strong an army in Ireland, and the Irish are become so much more cunning from the last insurrection, that you may perhaps be tolerably secure just at present from that evil : but are you secure from the efforts which the French may make to throw a body of troops into Ireland? and do you consider that event to be difficult and improbable? From Brest Harbour to Cape St. Vincent, you have above three thousand miles of hostile sea coast, and twelve or fourteen harbours quite capable of containing a sufficient force for the powerful invasion of Ireland. The nearest of these harbours is not two days' sail from the southern coast of Ireland, with a fair leading wind; and the furthest not ten. Five ships of the line, for so very short a passage, might carry five or six thousand troops with cannon and ammunition ; and Ireland presents to their attack a southern coast of more than

500 miles, abounding in deep bays, admirable harbours, and disaffected inhabitants. Your blockading ships may be forced to come home for provisions and repairs, or they may be blown off in a gale of wind and compelled to bear away for their own coast; and you will observe that the very same wind which locks you up in the British Channel, when you are got there, is evidently favourable for the invasion of Ireland. And yet this is called Government, and the people huzza Mr. Perceval for continuing to expose his country day after day to such tremendous perils as these; cursing the men who would have given up a question in theology to have saved us from such a risk. The British empire at this moment is in the state of a peach-blossom—if the wind blows gently from one quarter, it survives; if furiously from the other, it perishes. A stiff breeze may set in from the north, the Rochefort squadron will be taken, and the Minister will be the most holy of men: if it comes from some other point, Ireland is gone; we curse ourselves as a set of monastic madmen, and call out for the unavailing satisfaction of Mr. Perceval's head. Such a state of political existence is scarcely credible: it is the action of a mad young fool standing upon one foot, and peeping down the crater of Mount Ætna, not the conduct of a wise and sober people deciding upon their best and dearest interests: and in the name, the much-injured name, of heaven, what is it all for that

M

we expose ourselves to these dangers? Is it that we may sell more muslin? Is it that we may acquire more territory? Is it that we may strengthen what we have already acquired? No; nothing of all this; but that one set of Irishmen may torture another set of Irishmen—that Sir Phelim O'Callaghan may continue to whip Sir Toby M'Tackle, his next door neighbour, and continue to ravish his Catholic daughters; and these are the measures which the honest and consistent Secretary supports; and this is the Secretary whose genius in the estimation of Brother Abraham is to extinguish the genius of Bonaparte. Pompey was killed by a slave, Goliath smitten by a stripling. Pyrrhus died by the hand of a woman; tremble, thou great Gaul, from whose head an armed Minerva leaps forth in the hour of danger; tremble, thou scourge of God, a pleasant man is come out against thee, and thou shalt be laid low by a joker of jokes, and he shall talk his pleasant talk against thee, and thou shalt be no more!

You tell me, in spite of all this parade of sea-coast, Bonaparte has neither ships nor sailors: but this is a mistake. He has not ships and sailors to contest the empire of the seas with Great Britain, but there remains quite sufficient of the navies of France, Spain, Holland, and Denmark, for these short excursions and invasions. Do you think, too, that Bonaparte does not add to his navy every year? Do you

suppose, with all Europe at his feet, that he can find
any difficulty in obtaining timber, and that money will
not procure for him any quantity of naval stores he may
want? The mere machine, the empty ship, he can
build as well, and as quickly, as you can; and though
he may not find enough of practised sailors to man
large fighting-fleets—it is not possible to conceive
that he can want sailors for such sort of purposes as
I have stated. He is at present the despotic monarch
of above twenty thousand miles of sea-coast, and yet
you suppose he cannot procure sailors for the invasion
of Ireland. Believe, if you please, that such a fleet
met at sea by any number of our ships at all compar-
able to them in point of force, would be immediately
taken, let it be so; I count nothing upon their power
of resistance, only upon their power of escaping un-
observed. If experience has taught us anything, it is
the impossibility of perpetual blockades. The instances
are innumerable, during the course of this war, where
whole fleets have sailed in and out of harbour, in
spite of every vigilance used to prevent it. I shall
only mention those cases where Ireland is concerned.
In December, 1796, seven ships of the line, and ten
transports, reached Bantry Bay from Brest, without
having seen an English ship in their passage. It
blew a storm when they were off shore, and therefore
England still continues to be an independent kingdom. You will observe that at the very time the

French fleet sailed out of Brest Harbour, Admiral
Colpoys was cruising off there with a powerful
squadron, and still, from the particular circumstances
of the weather, found it impossible to prevent the
French from coming out.   During the time that
Admiral Colpoys was cruising off Brest, Admiral
Richery, with six ships of the line, passed him, and
got safe into the harbour.   At the very moment when
the French squadron was lying in Bantry Bay, Lord
Bridport with his fleet was locked up by a foul wind
in the Channel, and for several days could not stir to
the assistance of Ireland.   Admiral Colpoys, totally
unable to find the French fleet, came home.   Lord
Bridport, at the change of the wind, cruised for them
in vain, and they got safe back to Brest, without
having seen a single one of those floating bulwarks,
the possession of which we believe will enable us
with impunity to set justice and common sense at
defiance.   Such is the miserable and precarious state
of an anemocracy, of a people who put their trust in
hurricanes, and are governed by wind.   In August,
1798, three forty-gun frigates landed 1100 men
under Humbert, making the passage from Rochelle
to Killala without seeing any English ship.   In
October of the same year, four French frigates
anchored in Killala Bay with 2000 troops ; and
though they did not land their troops they returned
to France in safety.   In the same month, a line-of-

battle ship, eight stout frigates, and a brig, all full of troops and stores, reached the coast of Ireland, and were fortunately, in sight of land, destroyed, after an obstinate engagement, by Sir John Warren.

If you despise the little troop which, in these numerous experiments, did make good its landing, take with you, if you please, this *précis* of its exploits : eleven hundred men, commanded by a soldier raised from the ranks, put to rout a select army of 6000 men, commanded by General Lake, seized their ordnance, ammunition, and stores, advanced 150 miles into a country containing an armed force of 150,000 men, and at last surrendered to the Viceroy, an experienced general, gravely and cautiously advancing at the head of all his chivalry and of an immense army to oppose him. You must excuse these details about Ireland, but it appears to me to be of all other subjects the most important. If we conciliate Ireland, we can do nothing amiss ; if we do not, we can do nothing well. If Ireland was friendly, we might equally set at defiance the talents of Bonaparte and the blunders of his rival, Mr. Canning ; we could then support the ruinous and silly bustle of our useless expeditions, and the almost incredible ignorance of our commercial orders in council. Let the present administration give up but this one point, and there is nothing which I would not consent to grant them. Mr. Perceval shall have full liberty to insult the tomb of Mr. Fox, and to torment every eminent Dissenter in Great Britain; Lord Camden shall have large boxes of plums; Mr. Rose receive permission to prefix to his name the appellative of virtuous; and to the Viscount Castlereagh a round sum of ready money shall be well and truly paid into his hand. Lastly, what remains to Mr. George Canning, but that he ride up and down Pall Mall glorious upon a white horse, and that they cry out before him, Thus shall it be done to the statesman who hath written 'The Needy Knife-Grinder,' and the German play? Adieu only for the present; you shall soon hear from me again; it is a subject upon which I cannot long be silent.

LETTER IX

DEAR ABRAHAM—No Catholic can be chief Governor or Governor of this kingdom, Chancellor or Keeper of the Great Seal, Lord High Treasurer, Chief of any of the Courts of Justice, Chancellor of the Exchequer, Puisne Judge, Judge in the Admiralty, Master of the Rolls, Secretary of State, Keeper of the Privy Seal, Vice-Treasurer or his Deputy, Teller or Cashier of Exchequer, Auditor or General, Governor or Custos Rotulorum of Counties, Chief Governor's Secretary, Privy Councillor, King's Counsel, Serjeant, Attorney, Solicitor-General, Master in Chancery, Provost or Fellow of Trinity College, Dublin, Postmaster-General,

Master and Lieutenant-General of Ordnance, Com-
mander-in-Chief, General on the Staff, Sheriff, Sub-
Sheriff, Mayor, Bailiff, Recorder, Burgess, or any other
officer in a City, or a Corporation.   No Catholic can
be guardian to a Protestant, and no priest guardian at
all; no Catholic can be a gamekeeper, or have for
sale, or otherwise, any arms or warlike stores; no
Catholic can present to a living, unless he choose to
turn Jew in order to obtain that privilege; the pecuniary qualification of Catholic jurors is made higher
than that of Protestants, and no relaxation of the
ancient rigorous code is permitted, unless to those
who shall take an oath prescribed by 13 and 14
George III.   Now if this is not picking the plums
out of the pudding and leaving the mere batter to the
Catholics, I know not what is.   If it were merely the
Privy Council, it would be (I allow) nothing but a
point of honour for which the mass of Catholics were
contending, the honour of being chief-mourners or
pall-bearers to the country; but surely no man will
contend that every barrister may not speculate upon
the possibility of being a Puisne Judge; and that
every shopkeeper must not feel himself injured by his
exclusion from borough offices.

One of the greatest practical evils which the
Catholics suffer in Ireland is their exclusion from the
offices of Sheriff and Deputy Sheriff.   Nobody who is
unacquainted with Ireland can conceive the obstacles

which this opposes to the fair administration of justice. The formation of juries is now entirely in the hands of the Protestants; the lives, liberties, and properties of the Catholics in the hands of the juries; and this is the arrangement for the administration of justice in a country where religious prejudices are inflamed to the greatest degree of animosity! In this country, if a man be a foreigner, if he sell slippers, and sealing wax, and artificial flowers, we are so tender of human life that we take care half the number of persons who are to decide upon his fate should be men of similar prejudices and feelings with himself: but a poor Catholic in Ireland may be tried by twelve Percevals, and destroyed according to the manner of that gentleman in the name of the Lord, and with all the insulting forms of justice. I do not go the length of saying that deliberate and wilful injustice is done. I have no doubt that the Orange Deputy Sheriff thinks it would be a most unpardonable breach of his duty if he did not summon a Protestant panel. I can easily believe that the Protestant panel may conduct themselves very conscientiously in hanging the gentlemen of the crucifix; but I blame the law which does not guard the Catholic against the probable tenor of those feelings which must unconsciously influence the judgments of mankind. I detest that state of society which extends unequal degrees of protection to different creeds and persuasions; and I cannot describe to you the contempt I feel for a man who, calling himself a statesman, defends a system which fills the heart of every Irishman with treason, and makes his allegiance prudence, not choice.

I request to know if the vestry taxes in Ireland are a mere matter of romantic feeling which can affect only the Earl of Fingal? In a parish where there are four thousand Catholics and fifty Protestants, the Protestants may meet together in a vestry meeting at which no Catholic has the right to vote, and tax all the lands in the parish 1s. 6d. per acre, or in the pound, I forget which, for the repairs of the church —and how has the necessity of these repairs been ascertained? A Protestant plumber has discovered that it wants new leading; a Protestant carpenter is convinced the timbers are not sound; and the glazier who hates holy water (as an accoucheur hates celibacy, because he gets nothing by it) is employed to put in new sashes.

The grand juries in Ireland are the great scene of jobbing. They have a power of making a county rate to a considerable extent for roads, bridges, and other objects of general accommodation. 'You suffer the road to be brought through my park, and I will have the bridge constructed in a situation where it will make a beautiful object to your house. You do my job, and I will do yours.' These are the sweet and interesting subjects which occasionally occupy Milesian gentlemen while they are attendant upon this grand inquest of justice. But there is a religion, it seems, even in jobs; and it will be highly gratifying to Mr. Perceval to learn that no man in Ireland who believes in seven sacraments can carry a public road, or bridge, one yard out of the direction most beneficial to the public, and that nobody can cheat the public who does not expound the Scriptures in the purest and most orthodox manner. This will give pleasure to Mr. Perceval: but, from his unfairness upon these topics I appeal to the justice and the proper feelings of Mr. Huskisson. I ask him if the human mind can experience a more dreadful sensation than to see its own jobs refused, and the jobs of another religion perpetually succeeding? I ask him his opinion of a jobless faith, of a creed which dooms a man through life to a lean and plunderless integrity. He knows that human nature cannot and will not bear it; and if we were to paint a political Tartarus, it would be an endless series of snug expectations and cruel disappointments. These are a few of many dreadful inconveniences which the Catholics of all ranks suffer from the laws by which they are at present oppressed. Besides, look at human nature: what is the history of all professions? Joel is to be brought up to the bar: has Mrs. Plymley the slightest doubt of his being Chancellor? Do not his two shrivelled aunts live in the certainty of seeing him in that situation, and of cutting out with their own hands his equity habiliments? And I could name a certain minister of the Gospel who does not, in the bottom of his heart, much differ from these opinions. Do you think that the fathers and mothers of the holy Catholic Church are not as absurd as Protestant papas and mammas? The probability I admit to be, in each particular case, that the sweet little blockhead will in fact never get a brief;—but I will venture to say there is not a parent from the Giant's Causeway to Bantry Bay who does not conceive that his child is the unfortunate victim of the exclusion, and that nothing short of positive law could prevent his own dear, pre-eminent Paddy from rising to the highest honours of the State. So with the army and parliament; in fact, few are excluded; but, in imagination, all: you keep twenty or thirty Catholics out, and you lose the affections of four millions; and, let me tell you, that recent circumstances have by no means tended to diminish in the minds of men that hope of elevation beyond their own rank which is so congenial to our nature: from pleading for John Roe to taxing John Bull, from jesting for Mr. Pitt and writing in the *Anti-Jacobin*, to managing the affairs of Europe— these are leaps which seem to justify the fondest dreams of mothers and of aunts.

I do not say that the disabilities to which the Catholics are exposed amount to such intolerable grievances, that the strength and industry of a nation are overwhelmed by them : the increasing prosperity of Ireland fully demonstrates to the contrary. But I repeat again, what I have often stated in the course of our correspondence, that your laws against the Catholics are exactly in that state in which you have neither the benefits of rigour nor of liberality : every law which prevented the Catholic from gaining strength and wealth is repealed ; every law which can irritate remains ; if you were determined to insult the Catholics you should have kept them weak ; if you resolved to give them strength, you should have ceased to insult them—at present your conduct is pure, unadulterated folly.

Lord Hawkesbury says, 'We heard nothing about the Catholics till we began to mitigate the laws against them ; when we relieved them in part from this oppression they began to be disaffected.' This is very true ; but it proves just what I have said, that you have either done too much or too little ; and as there lives not, I hope, upon earth, so depraved a courtier that he would load the Catholics with their ancient chains, what absurdity it is, then, not to render their dispositions friendly, when you leave their arms and legs free !

You know, and many Englishmen know, what passes in China ; but nobody knows or cares what passes in Ireland. At the beginning of the present

Peter Plymley's Letters 173

reign no Catholic could realise property, or carry on
any business; they were absolutely annihilated, and
had no more agency in the country than so many
trees. They were like Lord Mulgrave's eloquence
and Lord Camden's wit; the legislative bodies did
not know of their existence. For these twenty-five
years last past the Catholics have been engaged in
commerce; within that period the commerce of
Ireland has doubled—there are four Catholics at
work for one Protestant, and eight Catholics at work
for one Episcopalian. Of course, the proportion
which Catholic wealth bears to Protestant wealth is
every year altering rapidly in favour of the Catholics.
I have already told you what their purchases of land
were the last year: since that period I have been at
some pains to find out the actual state of the Catholic
wealth: it is impossible upon such a subject to arrive
at complete accuracy; but I have good reason to
believe that there are at present 2000 Catholics in
Ireland possessing an income of £500 and upwards,
many of these with incomes of one, two, three, and
four thousand, and some amounting to fifteen and
twenty thousand per annum:—and this is the kingdom, and these the people, for whose conciliation we
are to wait Heaven knows when, and Lord Hawkesbury why! As for me, I never think of the situation
of Ireland without feeling the same necessity for
immediate interference as I should do if I saw blood

flowing from a great artery. I rush towards it with the instinctive rapidity of a man desirous of preventing death, and have no other feeling but that in a few seconds the patient may be no more.

I could not help smiling, in the times of No Popery, to witness the loyal indignation of many persons at the attempt made by the last ministry to do something for the relief of Ireland. The general cry in the country was, that they would not see their beloved Monarch used ill in his old age, and that they would stand by him to the last drop of their blood. I respect good feelings, however erroneous be the occasions on which they display themselves ; and therefore I saw in all this as much to admire as to blame. It was a species of affection, however, which reminded me very forcibly of the attachment displayed by the servants of the Russian ambassador at the beginning of the last century. His Excellency happened to fall down in a kind of apoplectic fit, when he was paying a morning visit in the house of an acquaintance. The confusion was of course very great, and messengers were despatched in every direction to find a surgeon : who, upon his arrival, declared that his Excellency must be immediately blooded, and prepared himself forthwith to perform the operation : the barbarous servants of the embassy, who were there in great numbers, no sooner saw the surgeon prepared to wound the arm of their master

with a sharp, shining instrument, than they drew their
swords, put themselves in an attitude of defence, and
swore in pure Sclavonic, 'that they would murder any
man who attempted to do him the slightest injury :
he had been a very good master to them, and they
would not desert him in his misfortunes, or suffer his
blood to be shed while he was off his guard, and
incapable of defending himself.' By good fortune,
the secretary arrived about this period of the dispute,
and his Excellency, relieved from superfluous blood
and perilous affection, was, after much difficulty,
restored to life.

There is an argument brought forward with some
appearance of plausibility in the House of Commons,
which certainly merits an answer : You know that the
Catholics now vote for members of parliament in
Ireland, and that they outnumber the Protestants in a
very great proportion ; if you allow Catholics to sit
in parliament, religion will be found to influence votes
more than property, and the greater part of the 100
Irish members who are returned to parliament will be
Catholics. Add to these the Catholic members who
are returned in England, and you will have a phalanx
of heretical strength which every minister will be compelled to respect, and occasionally to conciliate by
concessions incompatible with the interests of the
Protestant Church. The fact is, however, that you
are at this moment subjected to every danger of this

kind which you can possibly apprehend hereafter.   If
the spiritual interests of the voters are more powerful
than their temporal interests, they can bind down their
representatives to support any measures favourable to
the Catholic religion, and they can change the objects
of their choice till they have found Protestant members (as they easily may do) perfectly obedient to
their wishes.   If the superior possessions of the Protestants prevent the Catholics from uniting for a
common political object, then danger you fear
cannot exist : if zeal, on the contrary, gets the
better of acres, then the danger at present exists, from
the right of voting already given to the Catholics, and
it will not be increased by allowing them to sit in
parliament.   There are, as nearly as I can recollect,
thirty seats in Ireland for cities and counties, where
the Protestants are the most numerous, and where the
members returned must of course be Protestants.   In
the other seventy representations the wealth of the
Protestants is opposed to the number of the Catholics ;
and if all the seventy members returned were of the
Catholic persuasion, they must still plot the destruction of our religion in the midst of 588 Protestants.
Such terrors would disgrace a cook-maid, or a tooth-
less aunt—when they fall from the lips of bearded
and senatorial men, they are nauseous, antiperistaltic,
and emetical.

How can you for a moment doubt of the rapid

effects which would be produced by the emancipation? In the first place, to my certain knowledge the Catholics have long since expressed to his Majesty's Ministers their perfect readiness *to vest in his Majesty, either with the consent of the Pope, or without it if it cannot be obtained, the nomination of the Catholic prelacy.* The Catholic prelacy in Ireland consists of twenty-six bishops and the warden of Galway, a dignitary enjoying Catholic jurisdiction. The number of Roman Catholic priests in Ireland exceeds one thousand. The expenses of his peculiar worship are, to a substantial farmer or mechanic, five shillings per annum; to a labourer (where he is not entirely excused) one shilling per annum; this includes the contribution of the whole family, and for this the priest is bound to attend them when sick, and to confess them when they apply to him; he is also to keep his chapel in order, to celebrate divine service, and to preach on Sundays and holydays. In the northern district a priest gains from £30 to £50; in the other parts of Ireland from £60 to £90 per annum. The best paid Catholic bishops receive about £400 per annum; the others from £300 to £350. My plan is very simple: I would have 300 Catholic parishes at £100 per annum, 300 at £200 per annum, and 400 at £300 per annum; this, for the whole thousand parishes, would amount to £190,000. To the prelacy I would allot £20,000 in unequal proportions, from £1000 to £500; and I would appropriate £40,000 more for the support of Catholic Schools, and the repairs of Catholic churches; the whole amount of which sum is £250,000, about the expense of three days of one of our genuine, good English *just and necessary wars.* The clergy should all receive their salaries at the Bank of Ireland, and I would place the whole patronage in the hands of the Crown. Now, I appeal to any human being, except Spencer Perceval, Esq., of the parish of Hampstead, what the disaffection of a clergy would amount to, gaping after this graduated bounty of the Crown, and whether Ignatius Loyola himself, if he were a living blockhead instead of a dead saint, could withstand the temptation of bouncing from £100 a year at Sligo, to £300 in Tipperary? This is the miserable sum of money for which the merchants and landowners and nobility of England are exposing themselves to the tremendous peril of losing Ireland. The sinecure places of the Roses and the Percevals, and the 'dear and near relations,' put up to auction at thirty years' purchase, would almost amount to the money.

I admit that nothing can be more reasonable than to expect that a Catholic priest should starve to death, genteelly and pleasantly, for the good of the Protestant religion; but is it equally reasonable to expect that he should do so for the Protestant pews, and Protestant brick and mortar? On an Irish Sabbath

the bell of a neat parish church often summons to
church only the parson and an occasionally conform-
ing clerk; while, two hundred yards off, a thousand
Catholics are huddled together in a miserable hovel,
and pelted by all the storms of heaven. Can anything be more distressing than to see a venerable
man pouring forth sublime truths in tattered breeches,
and depending for his food upon the little offal he
gets from his parishioners? I venerate a human
being who starves for his principles, let them be what
they may; but starving for anything is not at all to
the taste of the honourable flagellants : strict principles, and good pay, is the motto of Mr. Perceval :
the one he keeps in great measure for the faults of
his enemies, the other for himself.

There are parishes in Connaught in which a Protestant was never settled nor even seen. In that
province, in Munster, and in parts of Leinster, the
entire peasantry for sixty miles are Catholics ; in these
tracts the churches are frequently shut for want of a
congregation, or opened to an assemblage of from six
to twenty persons. Of what Protestants there are in
Ireland, the greatest part are gathered together in
Ulster, or they live in towns. In the country of the
other three provinces the Catholics see no other
religion but their own, and are at the least as fifteen
to one Protestant. In the diocese of Tuam they are
sixty to one ; in the parish of St. Mulins, diocese of

Leghlin, there are four thousand Catholics and one
Protestant; in the town of Grasgenamana, in the
county of Kilkenny, there are between four and five
hundred Catholic houses, and three Protestant houses.
In the parish of Allen, county Kildare, there is no
Protestant, though it is very populous. In the parish
of Arlesin, Queen's County, the proportion is one
hundred to one. In the whole county of Kilkenny,
by actual enumeration, it is seventeen to one; in the
diocese of Kilmacduagh, province of Connaught,
fifty-two to one, by ditto. These I give you as a few
specimens of the present state of Ireland; and yet
there are men impudent and ignorant enough to
contend that such evils require no remedy, and that
mild family man who dwelleth in Hampstead can find
none but the cautery and the knife.

> ———'Omne per ignem
> Excoquitur vitium.'

I cannot describe the horror and disgust which
I felt at hearing Mr. Perceval call upon the then
Ministry for measures of vigour in Ireland. If I lived
at Hampstead upon stewed meats and claret; if I
walked to church every Sunday before eleven young
gentlemen of my own begetting, with their faces
washed, and their hair pleasingly combed; if the
Almighty had blessed me with every earthly comfort
—how awfully would I pause before I sent forth the
flame and the sword over the cabins of the poor,

brave, generous, open-hearted peasants of Ireland!
How easy it is to shed human blood; how easy it is
to persuade ourselves that it is our duty to do so,
and that the decision has cost us a severe struggle;
how much in all ages have wounds and shrieks and
tears been the cheap and vulgar resources of the rulers
of mankind; how difficult and how noble it is to
govern in kindness and to found an empire upon the
everlasting basis of justice and affection! But what
do men call vigour? To let loose hussars and to
bring up artillery, to govern with lighted matches, and
to cut, and push, and prime; I call this not vigour,
but the *sloth of cruelty and ignorance.* The vigour I
love consists in finding out wherein subjects are
aggrieved, in relieving them, in studying the temper
and genius of a people, in consulting their prejudices,
in selecting proper persons to lead and manage them,
in the laborious, watchful, and difficult task of increasing public happiness by allaying each particular
discontent. In this way Hoche pacified La Vendée
—and in this way only will Ireland ever be subdued.
But this, in the eyes of Mr. Perceval, is imbecility
and meanness. Houses are not broken open, women
are not insulted, the people seem all to be happy;
they are not rode over by horses, and cut by whips.
Do you call this vigour? Is this government?

VI.—'LETTER TO THE JOURNEYMEN AND LABOURERS OF ENGLAND, WALES, SCOTLAND, AND IRELAND. LETTER TO JACK HARROW.'

By William Cobbett

(Although Cobbett produced not a few political pamphlets in the strictest sense of the term, the infinitely greater part of his work is comprised during his earlier days in the volumes of Peter Porcupine's Gazette, *during his later in those of the* Weekly Register. *This latter, however, he himself for a time actually entitled* The Weekly Political Pamphlet, *while he alluded to it under that name even at other times; and his whole work was imbued even more deeply than that of Defoe with the pamphlet character. I have selected two examples from the critical time when he was still exasperated by his imprisonment, and stung into fresh efforts by debt and the prospect of fresh difficulties. They exhibit in the most striking form all Cobbett's pet*

hatreds—of the unreformed Parliament, of paper money, of political economy, of potatoes, and of many other things. The first is the Register *of 2d November* 1816, *the first number of the cheapened form, which was sold at twopence, and so acquired the name of* '*Twopenny Trash,*' *from a phrase of, as some say, Canning's, others Castlereagh's. The second is an early number of the papers written from America. They will, with the notes, explain themselves.*)

LETTER TO THE JOURNEYMEN AND LABOURERS OF ENGLAND, WALES, SCOTLAND, AND IRELAND, ON THE CAUSE OF THEIR PRESENT MISERIES: ON THE MEASURES WHICH HAVE PRODUCED THAT CAUSE ; ON THE REMEDIES WHICH SOME FOOLISH AND SOME CRUEL AND INSOLENT MEN HAVE PROPOSED ; AND ON THE LINE OF CONDUCT WHICH JOURNEYMEN AND LABOURERS OUGHT TO PURSUE, IN ORDER TO OBTAIN EFFECTUAL RELIEF, AND TO ASSIST IN PROMOTING THE TRANQUILLITY AND RESTORING THE HAPPINESS OF THEIR COUNTRY.

FRIENDS AND FELLOW-COUNTRYMEN—Whatever the pride of rank, of riches, or of scholarship may have induced some men to believe, or to affect to believe, the real strength and all the resources of a country

ever have sprung and ever must spring from the
labour of its people ; and hence it is that this nation,
which is so small in numbers and so poor in climate
and soil compared with many others, has, for many
ages, been the most powerful nation in the world : it
is the most industrious, the most laborious, and,
therefore, the most powerful.   Elegant dresses, superb
furniture, stately buildings, fine roads and canals, fleet
horses and carriages, numerous and stout ships, ware-
houses teeming with goods ; all these, and many other
objects that fall under our view, are so many marks
of national wealth and resources.   But all these
spring from *labour*.   Without the journeyman and
the labourer none of them could exist ; without the
assistance of their hands the country would be a
wilderness, hardly worth the notice of an invader.

As it is the labour of those who toil which makes
a country abound in resources, so it is the same class
of men, who must, by their arms, secure its safety
and uphold its fame.   Titles and immense sums of
money have been bestowed upon numerous Naval
and Military Commanders.   Without calling the
justice of these in question, we may assert that the
victories were obtained by *you* and your fathers and
brothers and sons, in co-operation with those Commanders, who, with *your* aid, have done great and
wonderful things ; but who, without that aid, would
have been as impotent as children at the breast.

With this correct idea of your own worth in your minds, with what indignation must you hear yourselves called the Populace, the Rabble, the Mob, the Swinish Multitude ; and with what greater indignation, if possible, must you hear the projects of those cool and cruel and insolent men, who, now that you have been, without any fault of yours, brought into a state of misery, propose to narrow the limit of parish relief, to prevent you from marrying in the days of your youth, or to thrust you out to seek your bread in foreign lands, never more to behold your parents or friends ? But suppress your indignation, until we return to this topic, after we have considered the *cause* of your present misery, and the measures which have produced that cause.

The times in which we live are full of peril. The nation, as described by the very creatures of Government, is fast advancing to that period when an important change must take place. It is the lot of mankind that some shall labour with their limbs and others with their minds ; and, on all occasions, more especially on an occasion like the present, it is the duty of the latter to come to the assistance of the former. We are all equally interested in the peace and happiness of our common country. It is of the utmost importance that, in the seeking to obtain these objects, our endeavours should be uniform, and tend all to the same point. Such an uniformity cannot

exist without an uniformity of sentiment as to public
matters, and to produce this latter uniformity amongst
you is the object of this address.

As to the cause of our present miseries, it is the
enormous amount of the taxes which the Government
compels us to pay for the support of its army, its placemen, its pensioners, etc., and for the payment of the
interest of its debt.   That this is the *real* cause has
been a thousand times proved; and it is now so
acknowledged by the creatures of the Government
themselves.   Two hundred and five of the Correspondents of the Board of Agriculture ascribe the
ruin of the country to taxation.   Numerous writers,
formerly the friends of the Pitt system, now declare
that taxation has been the cause of our distress.
Indeed, when we compare our present state to the
state of the country previous to the wars against
France, we must see that our present misery is owing
to no other cause.   The taxes then annually raised
amounted to about fifteen millions : they amounted
last year to seventy millions.   The nation was then
happy ; it is now miserable.

The writers and speakers who labour in the cause
of corruption, have taken great pains to make the
labouring classes believe that *they* are *not taxed* ; that
the taxes which are paid by the landlords, farmers,
and tradesmen, do not affect you, the journeymen and
labourers ; and that the tax-makers have been very

lenient towards you. But, I hope that you see to the bottom of these things now. You must be sensible that if all your employers were totally ruined in one day, you would be wholly without employment and without bread; and, of course, in whatever degree your employers are deprived of their means, they must withhold means from you. In America the most awkward common labourer receives five shillings a day, while provisions are cheaper in that country than in this. Here, a carter, boarded in the house, receives about seven pounds a year; in America, he receives about thirty pounds a year. What is it that makes this difference? Why, in America the whole of the taxes do not amount to more than about ten shillings a head upon the whole of the population; while in England they amount to nearly six pounds a head! *There*, a journeyman or labourer may support his family well, and save from thirty to sixty pounds a year: *here*, he amongst you is a lucky man, who can provide his family with food and with decent clothes to cover them, without any hope of possessing a penny in the days of sickness or of old age. *There*, the Chief Magistrate receives six thousand pounds a year; *here*, the civil list surpasses a million of pounds in amount, and as much is allowed to each of the Princesses in one year, as the chief magistrate of America receives in two years, though that country is nearly equal to this in population.

A Mr. Preston, a lawyer of great eminence, and a great praiser of Pitt, has just published a pamphlet, in which is this remark: 'It should always be remembered, that the eighteen pounds a year paid to any placeman or pensioner, withdraws from the public the means of giving active employment to one individual as the head of a family; thus depriving five persons of the means of sustenance from the fruits of honest industry and active labour, and rendering them paupers.' Thus this supporter of Pitt acknowledges the great truth that the taxes are the cause of a people's poverty and misery and degradation. We did not stand in need of this acknowledgment; the fact has been clearly proved before; but it is good for us to see the friends and admirers of Pitt brought to make this confession.

It has been attempted to puzzle you with this sort of question: 'If taxes be the cause of the people's misery, how comes it that they were not so miserable before the taxes were reduced as they are now?' Here is a fallacy which you will be careful to detect. I know that the taxes have been reduced; that is to say, *nominally* reduced, but not so in fact; on the contrary, they have, in reality, been greatly augmented. This has been done by the sleight-of-hand of paper money. Suppose, for instance, that four years ago, I had a hundred pounds to pay in taxes, then a hundred and thirty bushels of wheat would have paid my share. If I have now seventy-five pounds to pay in taxes, it will require a hundred and ninety bushels of wheat to pay my share of taxes. Consequently, though my taxes are nominally reduced, they are, in reality, greatly augmented. This has been done by the legerdemain of paper money. In 1812, the pound-note was worth only thirteen shillings in silver. It is now worth twenty shillings. Therefore, when we now pay a pound-note to the tax-gatherer, we really pay him twenty shillings where we before paid him thirteen shillings ; and the Landholders who lent pound-notes worth thirteen shillings each, are now paid their interest in pounds worth twenty shillings each. And the thing is come to what Sir Francis Burdett told the Parliament it would come to. He told them in 1811, that if they ever attempted to pay the interest of their debt in gold and silver, or in paper money equal in value to gold and silver, the farmers and tradesmen must be ruined, and the journeymen and labourers reduced to the last stage of misery.

Thus, then, it is clear that it is the weight of the taxes, under which you are sinking, which has already pressed so many of you down into the state of paupers, and which now threatens to deprive many of you of your existence. We next come to consider what have been the causes of this weight of taxes. Here we must go back a little in our history, and you will soon see that this intolerable weight has all proceeded from the want of a Parliamentary Reform.

In the year 1764, soon after the present king came to the throne, the annual interest of the Debt amounted to about five millions, and the whole of the taxes to about nine millions. But, soon after this, a war was entered on to compel the Americans to submit to be taxed by the Parliament, without being represented in that Parliament. The Americans triumphed, and, after the war was over, the annual interest of the Debt amounted to about nine millions, and the whole of the taxes to about fifteen millions. This was our situation when the French people began their Revolution. The French people had so long been the slaves of a despotic government, that the friends of freedom in England rejoiced at their emancipation. The cause of Reform, which had never ceased to have supporters in England for a great many years, now acquired new life, and the Reformers urged the Parliament to grant reform, instead of going to war against the people of France. The Reformers said : ' Give the nation reform, and you need fear no revolution.' The Parliament, instead of listening to the Reformers, crushed them, and went to war against the people of France ; and the consequence of these wars is, that the annual interest of the Debt now amounts to forty-five millions, and the whole of the taxes, during each of the last several years, to seventy millions. So that these wars have ADDED thirty-six millions a year to the interest of the Debt, and fifty-five millions a year to the amount of the whole of the taxes! This is the price that we have paid for having checked (for it is only checked) the progress of liberty in France; for having forced upon that people the family of Bourbon, and for having enabled another branch of that same family to restore the bloody Inquisition, which Napoleon had put down.

Since the restoration of the Bourbons and of the old Government of France has been, as far as possible, the grand result of the contest; since this has been the end of all our fightings and all our past sacrifices and present misery and degradation; let us see (for the inquiry is now very full of interest) what sort of Government that was which the French people had just destroyed, when our Government began its wars against that people.

If, only twenty-eight years ago, any man in England had said that the Government of France was one that ought to be suffered to exist, he would have been hooted out of any company. It is notorious that that Government was a cruel despotism; and that we and our forefathers always called it such. This description of that Government is to be found in all our histories, in all our Parliamentary debates, in all our books on Government and politics. It is notorious, that the family of Bourbon has produced the most perfidious and bloody monsters that ever disgraced the human form. It is notorious that millions of Frenchmen have been butchered, and burnt, and driven into exile by their commands.   It is recorded, even in the history of France, that one of them said that the putrid carcass of a Protestant smelt sweet to him. Even in these latter times, so late as the reign of Louis XIV., it is notorious that hundreds of thousands of innocent people were put to the most cruel death. In some instances, they were burnt in their houses; in others they were shut into lower rooms, while the incessant noise of kettle-drums over their heads, day and night, drove them to raving madness.   To enumerate all the infernal means employed by this tyrant to torture and kill the people, would fill a volume.   Exile was the lot of those who escaped the swords, the wheels, the axes, the gibbets, the torches of his hell-hounds.   England was the place of refuge for many of these persecuted people.   The grandfather of the present Earl of Radnor, and the father of the venerable Baron Maseres were amongst them; and it is well known that England owes no inconsiderable part of her manufacturing skill and industry to that atrocious persecution.   Enemies of freedom, wherever it existed, this family of Bourbon, in the reign of Louis XIV. and XV., fitted out expeditions for the purpose of restoring the Stuarts to the throne of England, and thereby caused great expense and bloodshed to this nation; and, even the Louis who was beheaded by his subjects, did, in the most perfidious manner, make war upon England, during her war with America. No matter what was the nature of the cause, his conduct was perfidious; he professed peace while he was preparing for war. His object could not be to assist freedom, because his own subjects were slaves.

Such was the family that were ruling in France when the French Revolution began. After it was resolved to go to war against the people of France, all the hirelings of corruption were set to work to gloss over the character and conduct of the old Government, and to paint in the most horrid colours the acts of vengeance which the people were inflicting on the numerous tyrants, civil, military, and ecclesiastical, whom the change of things had placed at their mercy. The people's turn was now come, and, in the days of their power, they justly bore in mind the oppressions which they and their forefathers had endured. The taxes imposed by the Government became at last intolerable. It had contracted a great debt to carry on its wars. In order to be able to pay the interest of this debt, and to support an enormous standing army in time of peace, it laid upon the people burdens which they could no longer endure. It fined and flogged fathers and mothers if their children were detected in smuggling. Its courts of justice were filled with cruel and base judges. The nobility treated the common people like dogs; these latter

o

were compelled to serve as soldiers, but were excluded from all share, or chance of honour and command, which were engrossed by the nobility.

Now, when the time came for the people to have the power in their hands, was it surprising that the first use they made of it was to take vengeance on their oppressors? I will not answer this question myself. It shall be answered by Mr. Arthur Young, the present Secretary of the Board of Agriculture. He was in France at the time, and living upon the very spot, and having examined into the causes of the Revolution, he wrote and published the following remarks, in his *Travels*, vol. i. page 603 :—

'It is impossible to justify the excesses of the people on their taking up arms ; they were certainly guilty of cruelties ; it is idle to deny the facts, for they have been proved too clearly to admit of doubt. But is it really the people to whom we are to impute the whole? Or to their oppressors, who had kept them so long in a state of bondage? He who chooses to be served by slaves and by ill-treated slaves, must know that he holds both his property and his life by a tenure far different from those who prefer the service of well-treated freemen ; and he who dines to the music of groaning sufferers, must not, in the moment of insurrection, complain that his sons' throats are cut. When such evils happen, they surely are more imputable to the tyranny of the master than to the cruelty of the servant. The analogy holds with the French peasants. The murder of a seigneur, or a country seat in flames, is recorded in every news-paper ; the rank of the person who suffers attracts notice ; but where do we find the registers of that seigneur's oppressions of his peasantry, and his exactions of feudal services from those whose children were dying around them for want of bread? Where do we find the minutes that assigned these starving wretches to some vile pettifogger, to be fleeced by impositions, and mockery of justice, in the seigneural courts? Who gives us the awards of the Intendant and his *sub-delegues*, which took off the taxes of a man of fashion, and laid them with accumulated weight on the poor, who were so unfortunate as to be his neighbours? Who has dwelt sufficiently upon explaining all the ramifications of despotism, regal, aristocratical, and ecclesiastical, pervading the whole mass of the people; reaching, like a circulating fluid, the most distant capillary tubes of poverty and wretchedness? In these cases the sufferers are too ignoble to be known; and the mass too indiscriminate to be pitied. But should a philosopher feel and reason thus? Should he mistake the cause for the effect? and, giving all his pity to the few, feel no compassion for the many, because they suffer in his eyes not individually but by millions? The excesses of the people cannot, I fear, be justified; it would undoubtedly have done them credit, both as men and as Christians, if they had possessed their new acquired power with moderation. But let it be remembered that the populace in no country ever use power with moderation; excess is inherent in their aggregate constitution: and as every Government in the world knows that violence infallibly attends power in such hands, it is doubly bound in common sense, and for common safety, so to conduct itself, that the people may not find an interest in public confusions. They will always suffer much and long, before they are effectually roused; nothing, therefore, can kindle the flame but such oppressions of some classes or order in society as give able men the opportunity of seconding the general mass; discontent will diffuse itself around; and if the Government take not warning in time, it is alone answerable for all the burnings and all the plunderings and all the devastation and all the blood that follow.'

Who can deny the justice of these observations? It was the Government alone that was justly charge-able with the excesses committed in this early stage, and, in fact, in every other stage, of the Revolution of France. If the Government had given way in time, none of these excesses would have been com-mitted. If it had listened to the complaints, the prayers, the supplications, the cries of the cruelly-treated and starving people; if it had changed its conduct, reduced its expenses, it might have been safe under the protection of the peace-officers, and might have disbanded its standing army. But it persevered; it relied upon the bayonet, and upon its judges and hangmen. The latter were destroyed, and the former went over to the side of the people. Was it any wonder that the people burnt the houses of their oppressors, and killed the owners and their families? The country contained thousands upon thousands of men that had been ruined by taxation, and by judgments of infamous courts of justice, 'a mockery of justice'; and, when these ruined men saw their oppressors at their feet, was it any wonder that they took vengeance upon them? Was it any wonder that the son, who had seen his father and mother flogged, because he, when a child, had smuggled a handful of salt, should burn for an occa-sion to shoot through the head the ruffians who had thus lacerated the bodies of his parents? Moses slew the insolent Egyptian who had smitten one of his countrymen in bondage. Yet Moses has never been called either a murderer or a cruel wretch for this act ; and the bondage of the Israelites was light as a feather compared to the tyranny under which the people of France had groaned for ages. Moses resisted oppression in the only way that resistance was in his power. He knew that his countrymen had no chance of justice in any court ; he knew that petitions against his oppressors were all in vain ; and 'looking upon the burdens' of his countrymen, he resolved to begin the only sort of resistance that was left him. Yet it was little more than a mere insult that drew forth his anger and resistance ; and, if Moses was justified, as he clearly was, what needs there any apology for the people of France ?

It seems at first sight very strange that the Government of France should not have 'taken warning in time.' But it had so long been in the habit of despising the people that its mind was incapable of entertaining any notion of danger from the oppressions heaped upon them. It was surrounded with panders and parasites who told it nothing but flattering falsehoods ; and it saw itself supported by two hundred and fifty thousand bayonets, which it thought irresistible ; though it found in the end that those who wielded those bayonets were not long so base as to be induced, either by threats or promises, to butcher their brothers and sisters and parents. And, if you ask me how it came to pass that they did not 'take warning in time,' I answer that they did take warning, but that, seeing that the change which was coming would deprive them of a great part of their power and emoluments, they resolved to resist the change, and to destroy the country, if possible, rather than not have all its wealth and power to themselves. The ruffian whom we read of, a little time ago, who stabbed a young woman because she was breaking from him to take the arm of another man whom she preferred, acted upon the principle of the ministers, the noblesse, and the clergy of France. They could no longer unjustly possess, therefore they would destroy. They saw that if a just government were established ; that if the people were fairly represented in a national council ; they saw that if this were to take place, they would no longer be able to wallow in wealth at the expense of the people ; and, seeing this, they resolved to throw all into confusion, and, if possible, to make a heap of ruins of that country which they could no longer oppress, and the substance of which they could no longer devour.

Talk of violence indeed ! Was there anything too violent, anything too severe to be inflicted on these men ? It was they who produced confusion ; it was they who caused the massacres and guillotinings ; it was they who destroyed the kingly government ; it was they who brought the king to the block. They were answerable for all and for every single part of the mischief, as much as Pharaoh was for the plagues in Egypt, which history of Pharaoh seems, by the bye, to be intended as a lesson to all future tyrants. He 'set taskmasters over the Israelites to afflict them with burdens; and he made them build treasure cities for him; he made them serve with rigour; he made their lives bitter with hard bondage, in mortar and in brick, and in all manner of service of the field; he denied them straw, and insisted upon their making the same quantity of bricks, and because they were unable to obey, the taskmasters called them idle and beat them.' Was it too much to scourge and to destroy all the first-born of men who could tolerate, assist, and uphold a tyrant like this? Yet was Pharaoh less an oppressor than the old government of France.

Thus, then, we have a view of the former state of that country, by wars against the people of which we have been brought into our present state of misery. There are many of the hirelings of corruption, who actually insist on it that we ought now to go to war again for the restoring of all the cruel despotism which formerly existed in France. This is what cannot be done, however. Our wars have sent back the Bourbons; but the tithes, the seigneurs, and many other curses have not been restored. The French people still enjoy much of the benefit of the Revolution ; and great numbers of their ancient petty tyrants have been destroyed. So that even were things to remain as they are, the French people have gained greatly by their Revolution. But things cannot remain as they are. Better days are at hand.

In proceeding now to examine the remedies for your distresses, I shall first notice some of those which foolish, or cruel and insolent men have proposed. Seeing that the cause of your misery is the weight of taxation, one would expect to hear of nothing but a reduction of taxation in the way of remedy ; but from the friends of corruption never do we hear of any such remedy. To hear them, one would think that *you* had been the guilty cause of the misery you suffer; and that you, and you alone, ought to be made answerable for what has taken place. The emissaries of corruption are now continually crying out against the weight of the Poor-rates, and they seem to regard all that is taken in that way as a dead loss to the Government ! Their project is to deny relief to all who are able to work. But what is the use of your being able to work, if no one will, or can, give you work ? To tell you that you must work for your bread, and, at the same time, not to find any work for you, is full as bad as it would be to order you to make bricks without straw. Indeed, it is rather more cruel and insolent; for Pharaoh's taskmasters did point out to the Israelites that they might go into the fields and get *stubble*. The *Courier* newspaper of the 9th of October, says, 'We must thus be cruel only to be kind.'   I am persuaded that you will not understand this kindness, while you will easily understand the cruelty.   The notion of these people seems to be that everybody that receives money out of the taxes has a right to receive it, except you.   They tremble at the fearful amount of the Poor-rates : they say, and very truly, that those rates have risen from two and a half to eight or ten millions since the beginning of the wars against the people of France ; they think, and not without reason, that these rates will soon swallow up nearly all the rent of the land.   These assertions and apprehensions are perfectly well founded ; but how can *you* help it ?   You have not had the management of the affairs of the nation.   It is not you who have ruined the farmers and tradesmen.   You only want food and raiment : you are ready to work for it ; but you cannot go naked and without food.

But the complaints of these persons against you are the more unreasonable, because they say not a word against the sums paid to sinecure placemen and pensioners.   Of the five hundred and more Correspondents of the Board of Agriculture, there are scarcely ten who do not complain of the weight of the Poor-rates, of the immense sums taken away from them by the poor, and many of them complain of the idleness of the poor.   But not one single man complains of the immense sums taken away to support sinecure placemen, who do nothing for their money, and to support pensioners, many of whom are women and children, the wives and daughters of the nobility and other persons in high life, and who can do nothing, and never can have done anything for what they receive. There are of these places and pensions all sizes, from twenty pounds to thirty thousand and nearly forty thousand pounds a year! And surely these ought to be done away before any proposition be made to take the parish allowance from any of you who are unable to work, or to find work to do. There are several individual placemen, the profits of each of which would maintain a thousand families. The names of the ladies upon the pension list would, if printed, one under another, fill a sheet of paper like this. And is it not, then, base and cruel at the same time in these Agricultural correspondents to cry out so loudly against the charge of supporting the unfortunate poor, while they utter not a word of complaint against the sinecure places and pensions?

The unfortunate journeymen and labourers and their families have a right, they have a just claim, to relief from the purses of the rich. For there can exist no riches and no resources which they by their labour have not assisted to create. But I should be glad to know how the sinecure placemen and lady pensioners have assisted to create food and raiment, or the means of producing them. The labourer who is out of work or ill, to-day, may be able to work, and set to work to-morrow. While those placemen and pensioners never can work; or, at least, it is clear that they never intend to do it.

You have been represented by the *Times* newspaper, by the *Courier*, by the *Morning Post*, by the *Morning Herald*, and others, as the *scum* of society. They say that you have no business at public meetings; that you are rabble, and that you pay no taxes. These insolent hirelings, who wallow in wealth, would not be able to put their abuse of you in print were it not for your labour. You create all that is an object of taxation; for even the land itself would be good for nothing without your labour. But are you not taxed? Do you pay no taxes? One of the correspondents of the Board of Agriculture has said that care has been taken to lay as little tax as possible on the articles used by you. One would wonder how a man could be found impudent enough to put an assertion like this upon paper. But the people of this country have so long been insulted by such men, that the insolence of the latter knows no bounds.

The tax gatherers do not, indeed, come to you and demand money of you: but there are few articles which you use, in the purchase of which you do not pay a tax.

On your shoes, salt, beer, malt, hops, tea, sugar, candles, soap, paper, coffee, spirits, glass of your windows, bricks and tiles, tobacco : on all these, and many other articles you pay a tax, and even on your loaf you pay a tax, because everything is taxed from which the loaf proceeds.   In several cases the tax amounts to more than one half of what you pay for the article itself; these taxes go in part to support sinecure placemen and pensioners ; and the ruffians of the hired press call you the scum of society, and deny that you have any right to show your faces at any public meeting to petition for a reform, or for the removal of any abuse whatever !

Mr. Preston, whom I quoted before, and who is a member of Parliament and has a large estate, says upon this subject, 'Every family, even of the poorest labourer, consisting of five persons, may be considered as paying, in indirect taxes, at least ten pounds a year, or more than half his wages at seven shillings a week!' And yet the insolent hirelings call you the mob, the rabble, the scum, the swinish multitude, and say that your voice is nothing ; that you have no business at public meetings ; and that you are, and ought to be considered as nothing in the body politic !   Shall we never see the day when these men will change their tone !   Will they never cease to look upon us [as on] brutes !   I trust they will change their tone, and that the day of the change is at no great distance !

The weight of the Poor-rate, which must increase while the present system continues, alarms the corrupt, who plainly see that what is paid to relieve you, they cannot have. Some of them, therefore, hint at your early marriages as a great evil, and a clergyman named Malthus has seriously proposed measures for checking you in this respect ; while one of the correspondents of the Board of Agriculture complains of the increase of bastards, and proposes severe punishment on the parents ! How hard these men are to please ! What would they have you do ? As some have called you the swinish multitude, would it be much wonder if they were to propose to serve you as families of young pigs are served ? Or if they were to bring forward the measure of Pharaoh, who ordered the midwives to kill all the male children of the Israelites ?

But, if you can restrain your indignation at these insolent notions and schemes, with what feelings must you look upon the condition of your country, where the increase of the people is now looked upon as a curse ! Thus, however, has it always been, in all countries where taxes have produced excessive misery. Our countryman, Mr. Gibbon, in his History of the *Decline and Fall of the Roman Empire*, has the following passage : 'The horrid practice of murdering their new-born infants was become every day more frequent in the provinces. It was the effect of *distress*, and the distress was principally occasioned by the *intolerable burden of taxes,* and by the vexatious as well as cruel prosecutions of the officers of the revenue against their insolvent debtors. The less opulent or less industrious part of mankind, instead of rejoicing at an increase of family, deemed it an act of paternal tenderness to release the children from the impending miseries of a life which they themselves were unable to support.'

But that which took place under the base Emperor Constantine will not take place in England. You will not murder your new-born infants, nor will you, to please the corrupt and insolent, debar yourselves from enjoyments to which you are invited by the very first of Nature's laws. It is, however, a disgrace to the country that men should be found in it capable of putting ideas so insolent upon paper. So, then, a young man arm-in-arm with a rosy-cheeked girl must be a spectacle of evil omen! What! and do they imagine that you are thus to be extinguished, because some of you are now (without any fault of yours) unable to find work? As far as you were wanted to labour, to fight, or to pay taxes, you were welcome, and they boasted of your numbers; but now that your country has been brought into a state of misery, these corrupt and insolent men are busied with schemes for getting rid of you. Just as if you had not as good a right to live and to love and to marry as they have! They do not propose, far from it, to check the breeding of sinecure placemen and pensioners, who are supported in part by the taxes which you help to pay. They say not a word about the whole families who are upon the pension list. In many cases there are sums granted in trust for *the children* of such a lord or such a lady. And while labourers and journeymen who have large families too, are actually paying taxes for the support of these lords' and ladies' children, these cruel and insolent men propose that they shall have no relief, and that their having children ought to be checked! To such a subject no words can do justice. You will feel as you ought to feel; and to the effect of your feelings I leave these cruel and insolent men.

There is one more scheme to notice, which, though rather less against nature is not less hateful and insolent; namely, to encourage you to emigrate to foreign countries. This scheme is distinctly proposed to the Government by one of the correspondents of the Board of Agriculture. What he means by encouragement must be to send away by force, or by paying for the passage; for a man who has money stands in no need of relief. But, I trust, that not a man of you will move, let the *encouragement* be what it may. It is impossible for many to go, though the prospect be ever so fair. We must stand by our country, and it is base not to stand by her, as long as there is a chance of seeing her what she ought to be. But the proposition is, nevertheless, base and insolent. This man did not propose to encourage the sinecure placemen and pensioners to emigrate; yet, surely, you who help to maintain them by the taxes which you pay, have as good a right to remain in the country as they have! You have fathers and mothers and sisters and brothers and children and friends as well as they; but this base projector recommends that you may be encouraged to leave your relations and friends for ever; while he would have the sinecure placemen and pensioners remain quietly where they are !

No: you will not leave your country. If you have suffered much and long, you have the greater right to remain in the hope of seeing better days. And I beseech you not to look upon yourselves as the *scum*; but, on the contrary, to be well persuaded that a great deal will depend upon your exertions; and therefore, I now proceed to point out to you what appears to me to be the line of conduct which journeymen and labourers ought to pursue in order to obtain effectual relief, and to assist in promoting tranquillity and restoring the happiness of the country.

We have seen that the cause of our miseries is the burden of taxes occasioned by wars, by standing armies, by sinecures, by pensions, etc. It would be endless and useless to enumerate all the different heads or sums of expenditure. The remedy is what we have now to look to, and that remedy consists wholly and solely of such a reform in the Commons' or People's House of Parliament, as shall give to every payer of direct taxes a vote at elections, and as shall cause the Members to be elected annually.

In a late *Register* I have pointed out how easily, how peaceably, how fairly, such a Parliament might be chosen. I am aware that it may, and not without justice, be thought wrong to deprive those of the right of voting who pay indirect taxes. Direct taxes are those which are directly paid by any person into the hands of the tax-gatherers, as the assessed rates and taxes. Indirect taxes are those which are paid indirectly through the maker or seller of goods, as the tax on soap or candles or salt or malt. And, as no man ought to be taxed without his consent, there has always been a difficulty upon this head. There has been no question about the *right* of every man who is free to exercise his will, who has a settled place in society, and who pays a tax of any sort, to vote for Members of Parliament. The difficulty is in taking the votes by any other means than by the Rate-book ; for if there be no list of tax-payers in the hands of any person, mere menial servants, vagrants, pickpockets, and scamps of all sorts might not only come to the poll, but they might poll in several parishes or places, on one and the same day. A corrupt rich man might employ scores of persons of this description, and in this way would the purpose of reform be completely defeated. In America, where one branch of the Congress is elected for four years and the other for two years, they have still adhered to the principle of direct taxation, and in some of the States they have made it necessary for a voter to be worth one hundred pounds. Yet they have, in that country, duties on goods, custom duties, and excise duties also ; and, of course, there are many persons who really pay taxes, and who, nevertheless, are not permitted to vote. The people do not complain of this. They know that the number of votes is so great that no corruption can take place, and they have no desire to see livery servants, vagrants, and pickpockets take part in their elections. Nevertheless it would be very easy for a reformed Parliament, when once it had taken root, to make a just arrangement of this matter. The most likely method would be to take off the indirect taxes, and to put a small direct tax upon every master of a house, however low his situation in life.

But this and all other good things, must be done by a reformed Parliament. We must have that first, or we shall have nothing good ; and any man who would beforehand take up your time with the detail of what a reformed Parliament ought to do in this respect, or with respect to any changes in the form of government, can have no other object than that of defeating the cause of reform; and, indeed, the very act must show, that to raise obstacles is his wish.

Such men, now that they find you justly irritated, would persuade you that, because things have been perverted from their true ends, there is nothing good in our constitution and laws. For what, then, did Hampden die in the field, and Sydney on the scaffold? And has it been discovered at last that England has always been an enslaved country from top to toe? The Americans, who are a very wise people, and who love liberty with all their hearts, and who take care to enjoy it too, took special care not to part with any of the great principles and laws which they derived from their forefathers. They took special care to speak with reverence of, and to preserve Magna Charta, the Bill of Rights, the Habeas Corpus, and not only all the body of the Common Law of England, but most of the rules of our courts, and all our form of jurisprudence. Indeed it is the greatest glory of England that she has thus supplied with sound principles of freedom those immense regions which will be peopled perhaps by hundreds of millions.

I know of no enemy of reform and of the happiness of the country so great as that man who would persuade you that we possess nothing good, and that all must be torn to pieces. There is no principle, no precedent, no regulations (except as to mere matter of detail), favourable to freedom, which is not to be found in the

Laws of England or in the example of our ancestors. Therefore I say we may ask for, and we want nothing new. We have great constitutional laws and principles to which we are immovably attached. We want great alteration, but we want nothing new. Alteration, modification, to suit the times and circumstances; but the great principles ought to be and must be the same, or else confusion will follow.

It was the misfortune of the French people that they had no great and settled principles to refer to in their laws or history. They sallied forth and inflicted vengeance on their oppressors; but, for want of settled principles to which to refer they fell into confusion; they massacred each other; they next flew to a military chief to protect them even against themselves; and the result has been what we too well know. Let us therefore congratulate ourselves that we have great constitutional principles and laws, to which we can refer, and to which we are attached.

That reform will come I know, if the people do their duty; and all that we have to guard against is confusion, which cannot come if reform take place in time. I have before observed to you that when the friends of corruption in France saw that they could not prevent a change, they bent their endeavours to produce confusion, in which they fully succeeded. They employed numbers of unprincipled men to go about the country proposing all sorts of mad schemes. They produced first a confusion in men's minds, and next a civil war between provinces, towns, villages and families. The tyrant Robespierre, who was exceeded in cruelty only by some of the Bourbons, was proved to have been in league with the open enemies of France. He butchered all the real friends of freedom whom he could lay his hands on, except Paine, whom he shut up in a dungeon till he was reduced to a skeleton. This monster was at last put to death himself; and his horrid end ought to be a warning to any man who may wish to walk in the same path. But I am, for my part, in little fear of the influence of such men. They cannot cajole you as Robespierre cajoled the people of Paris. It is, nevertheless, necessary for you to be on your guard against them, and when you hear a man talking big and hectoring about projects which go further than a real and radical reform of the Parliament, be you well assured that that man would be a second Robespierre if he could, and that he would make use of you and sacrifice the life of the very last man of you; that he would ride upon the shoulders of some through rivers of the blood of others, for the purpose of gratifying his own selfish and base and insolent ambition.

In order effectually to avoid the rock of confusion, we should keep steadily in our eye not only what we wish to be done but what can be done now. We know that such a reform as would send up a Parliament, chosen by all payers of direct taxes, is not only just and reasonable, but easy of execution. I am therefore for accomplishing that object first; and I am not at all afraid that a set of men who would really hold the purse of the people, and who had been just chosen freely by the people, would very soon do everything that the warmest friend of freedom could wish to see done.

While, however, you are upon your guard against false friends, you should neglect no opportunity of doing all that is within your power to give support to the cause of reform. Petition is the channel for your sentiments, and there is no village so small that its petition would not have some weight. You ought to attend at every public meeting within your reach. You ought to read to and to assist, each other in coming at a competent knowledge of all public matters. Above all things, you ought to be unanimous in your object, and not suffer yourselves to be divided.

The subject of religion has nothing to do with this great question of reform. A reformed Parliament would soon do away with all religious distinctions and disabilities. In their eyes, a Catholic and a Protestant would both appear in the same light.

The *Courier*, the *Times*, and other emissaries of corruption, are constantly endeavouring to direct your wrath against bakers, brewers, butchers, and other persons who deal in the necessaries of life. But, I trust that you are not to be stimulated to such a species of violence. These tradesmen are as much in distress as you. They cannot help their malt and hops and beer and bread and meat being too dear for you to purchase. They all sell as cheap as they can, without being absolutely ruined. The beer you drink is more than half *tax*, and when the tax has been paid by the seller he must have payment back again from you who drink, or he must be ruined. The baker has numerous taxes to pay, and so has the butcher, and so has the miller and the farmer. Besides, all men are eager to sell, and, if they could sell cheaper they certainly would, because that would be the sure way of getting more custom. It is the weight of the taxes which presses us all to the earth, except those who receive their incomes out of those taxes. Therefore I exhort you most earnestly not to be induced to lay violent hands on those who really suffer as much as yourselves.

On the subject of lowering wages too, you ought to consider that your employers cannot give to you that which they have not. At present, corn is high in price, but that high price is no benefit to the farmer, because it has risen from the badness of the crop, which Mr. Hunt foretold at the Common Hall, and for the foretelling of which he was so much abused by the hirelings of the press, who, almost up to this very moment, have been boasting and thanking God for the goodness of the crop ! The farmer whose corn is half destroyed, gains nothing by selling the remaining half for double the price at which he would have sold the whole. If I grow 10 quarters of wheat, and if I save it all and sell it for two pounds a quarter, I receive as much money as if I had sold the one-half of it for four pounds a quarter. And I am better off in the former case, because I want wheat for seed, and because I want some to consume myself. These matters I recommend to your serious consideration; because it being unjust to fall upon your employers to force them to give that which they have not to give, your conduct in such cases must tend to weaken the great cause in which we ought all now to be engaged, namely the removal of our burdens through the means of a reformed Parliament. It is the interest of vile men of all descriptions to set one part of the people against the other part; and therefore it becomes you to be constantly on your guard against their allurements.

When journeymen find their wages reduced, they should take time to reflect on the real cause, before they fly on their employers, who are in many cases in as great or greater distress than themselves. How many of those employers have of late gone to jail for debt and left helpless families behind them! The employer's trade falls off. His goods are reduced in price. His stock loses the half of its value. He owes money. He is ruined; and how can he continue to pay high wages? The cause of his ruin is the weight of the taxes, which presses so heavily on us all, that we lose the power of purchasing goods. But it is certain that a great many, a very large portion of the farmers, tradesmen, and manufacturers, have, by their supineness and want of public spirit, contributed towards the bringing of this ruin upon themselves and upon you. They have *skulked* from their public duty. They have kept aloof from, or opposed all measures for a redress of grievances; and indeed, they still skulk, though ruin and destruction stare them in the face. Why do they not now come forward and explain to you the real cause of the reduction of your wages? Why do they not put themselves at your head in petitioning for redress? This would secure their property much better than the calling in of troops, which can never afford them more than a short and precarious security. In the days of their prosperity they were amply warned of what has now come to pass; and the far greater part of them abused and calumniated those who gave them the warning. Even if they would now act the part of men worthy of being relieved, the relief to us all would speedily follow. If they will not; if they will still skulk, they will merit all the miseries which they are destined to suffer.

Instead of coming forward to apply for a reduction of those taxes which are pressing them as well as you to the earth, what are they doing? Why, they are applying to the Government to add to their receipts by passing Corn Bills, by preventing foreign wool from being imported; and many other silly schemes. Instead of asking for a reduction of taxes they are asking for the means of paying taxes! Instead of asking for the abolition of sinecure places and pensions, they pray to be enabled to continue to pay the amount of those places and pensions! They know very well that the salaries of the judges and of many other persons were greatly raised, some years ago, on the ground of the rise in the price of labour and provisions, why then do they not ask to have those salaries reduced, now that labour is reduced? Why do they not apply to the case of the judges and others the arguments which they apply to you? They can talk boldly enough to you; but they are too great cowards to talk to the Government, even in the way of petition! Far more honourable is it to be a ragged pauper than to be numbered among such men.

These people call themselves the *respectable* part of the nation. They are, as they pretend, the virtuous part of the people, because they are quiet; as if virtue consisted in immobility! There is a canting Scotchman in London, who publishes a paper called the ' *Champion*,' who is everlastingly harping upon the virtues of the ' fireside,' and who inculcates the duty of quiet submission. Might we ask this Champion of the teapot and milk-jug whether Magna Charta and the Bill of Rights were won by the fireside? Whether the tyrants of the House of Stuart

and of Bourbon were hurled down by fireside virtues?
Whether the Americans gained their independence,
and have preserved their freedom, by sitting by the fireside? O, no! these were all achieved by action, and
amidst bustle and noise. Quiet indeed! Why in
this quality a log, or a stone, far surpasses even the
pupils of this Champion of quietness; and the chairs
round his fireside exceed those who sit in them. But
in order to put these quiet, fireside, respectable people
to the test, let us ask them if they approve of drunken-
ness, breaches of the peace, black eyes, bloody noses,
fraud, bribery, corruption, perjury, and subornation of
perjury; and if they say no, let us ask them whether these
are not going on all over the country at every general
election. If they answer yes, as they must unless they
be guilty of wilful falsehood, will they then be so good
as to tell us how they reconcile their inactivity with
sentiments of virtue? Some men, in all former ages,
have been held in esteem for their wisdom, their genius,
their skill, their valour, their devotion to country, etc.,
but never until this age, was *quietness* deemed a quality
to be extolled. It would be no difficult matter to
show that the quiet, fireside gentry are the most callous
and cruel, and, therefore, the most wicked part of the
nation. Amongst them it is that you find all the
peculators, all the blood-suckers of various degrees, all
the borough-voters and their offspring, all the selfish
and unfeeling wretches, who, rather than risk the dis-

turbing of their ease for one single month, rather than
go a mile to hold up their hand at a public meeting, would see half the people perish with hunger and
cold. The humanity, which is continually on their lips,
is all fiction. They weep over the tale of woe in a
novel; but round their 'decent fireside,' never was
compassion felt for a real sufferer, or indignation at
the acts of a powerful tyrant.

The object of the efforts of such writers is clearly
enough seen. Keep all *quiet*! Do not rouse! Keep
still! Keep down! Let those who perish, perish in
silence! It will, however, be out of the power of these
quacks, with all their laudanum, to allay the blood
which is now boiling in the veins of the people of this
kingdom; who, if they are doomed to perish, are at
any rate resolved not to perish in silence. The
writer whom I have mentioned above, says that he,
of course, does not count 'the lower classes, who,
under the pressure of need or under the influence
of ignorant prejudice, may blindly and weakly rush
upon certain and prompt punishment; but that the
security of every decent fireside, every respectable
father's best hopes for his children, still connect themselves with the Government.' And by Government he
clearly means all the mass as it now stands. There is
nobody so callous and so insolent as your sentimental
quacks and their patients. How these 'decent fireside' people would stare, if some morning they were

to come down and find them occupied by uninvited
visitors ! I hope they never will. I hope that things
will never come to this pass : but if one thing more
than any other tends to produce so sad an effect, it is
the cool insolence with which such men as this writer
treats the most numerous and most suffering classes
of the people.

Long as this Address already is, I cannot conclude without some observations on the ' Charity Sub-
scriptions ' at the London Tavern. The object of this
subscription professes to be to afford relief to the distressed labourers, etc. About forty thousand pounds
have been subscribed, and there is no probability of
its going much further. There is an absurdity on the
face of the scheme ; for, as all parishes are compelled
by law to afford relief to every person in distress, it
is very clear that, as far as money is given by these
people to relieve the poor, there will be so much
saved in the parish rates. But the folly of the thing
is not what I wish you most to attend to. Several
of the subscribers to this fund receive each of them
more than ten thousand pounds and some more
than thirty thousand pounds each, out of those taxes
which you help to pay, and which emoluments not a
man of them proposes to give up. The clergy appear
very forward in this subscription. An Archbishop and
a Bishop assisted at the forming of the scheme. Now
then, observe that there has been given out of the taxes,

for several years past, one hundred thousand pounds a year, for what, think you? Why for the relief of the poor clergy! I have no account at hand later than that delivered last year, and there I find this sum!—for the poor clergy! The rich clergy do not pay this sum; but it comes out of those taxes, part, and a large part of which you pay on your beer, malt, salt, shoes, etc. I daresay that the 'decent firesides' of these poor clergy still connect themselves with the Government. Amongst all our misery we have had to support the intolerable disgrace of being an object of the charity of a Bourbon Prince, while we are paying for supporting that family upon the throne of France. Well! But is this all? We are taxed, at the very same moment, for the support of the French Emigrants! And you shall see to what amount. Nay, not only French, but Dutch and others, as appears from the forementioned account laid before Parliament last year. The sum, paid out of the taxes, in one year, for the relief of suffering French Clergy and Laity, St. Domingo Sufferers, Dutch Emigrants, Corsican Emigrants, was one hundred and eighty-seven thousand seven hundred and fifty pounds; yes, one hundred and eighty-seven thousand seven hundred and fifty pounds paid to this set in one year out of those taxes of which you pay so large a share, while you are insulted with a subscription to relieve you, and while there are projectors who have the audacity to recommend schemes for preventing you from marrying while young, and to induce you to emigrate from your country! I'll venture my life that the ' decent firesides ' of all this swarm of French clergy and laity, and Dutch, and Corsicans, and St. Domingo sufferers 'still connect themselves closely with the Government'; and I will also venture my life that you do not stand in need of one more word to warm every drop of blood remaining in your bodies ! As to the money subscribed by regiments of soldiers, whose pay arises from taxes in part paid by you, though it is a most shocking spectacle to behold, I do not think so much of it. The soldiers are your fathers, brothers, and sons. But if they were all to give their whole pay, and if they amount to one hundred and fifty thousand men, it would not amount to one-half of what is now paid in Poor-rates, and of course would not add half a pound of bread to every pound which the unhappy paupers now receive. All the expenses of the Army and Ordnance amount to an enormous sum—to sixteen or eighteen millions; but the pay of one hundred and fifty thousand men, at a shilling a day each, amounts to no more than two million seven hundred and twelve thousand five hundred pounds. So that, supposing them all to receive a shilling a day each, the soldiers receive only about a third part of the sum now paid annually in Poor-rates.

I have no room, nor have I any desire, to appeal to your passions upon this occasion. I have laid before you, with all the clearness I am master of, the causes of our misery, the measures which have led to those causes, and I have pointed out what appears to me to be the only remedy—namely a reform of the Commons', or People's House of Parliament. I exhort you to proceed in a peaceable and lawful manner, but at the same time to proceed with zeal and resolution in the attainment of this object. If the skulkers will not join you, if the 'decent fireside' gentry still keep aloof, proceed by yourselves. Any man can draw up a petition, and any man can carry it up to London, with instructions to deliver it into trusty hands, to be presented whenever the House shall meet. Some further information will be given as to this matter in a future Number. ⸺ In the meanwhile, I remain your Friend, WM. COBBETT.

TO JACK HARROW, AN ENGLISH LABOURER

On the new Cheat which is now on foot, and which goes under the name of Savings Banks

NORTH HAMPSTEAD, LONG ISLAND,
November 7th, 1818.

FRIEND JACK—You sometimes hear the Parson talk about deceivers, who go about in sheep's clothing; but who inwardly are ravening wolves. You frequently hear of the tricks of the London cheats, and I daresay you have often enough witnessed those of mounte-banks and gypsies. But, Jack, all the tricks of these deceivers and cheaters, if the trickery of them all were put together, would fall far short of the trick now playing off under the name of Savings Banks. And seeing that it is possible that you may be exposed to the danger of having a few pounds picked out of your pocket by this trick, I think it right to put you on your guard against the cheat.

You have before been informed of who and what the Boroughmongers are. Therefore, at present, I shall enter into no explanation of their recent conduct. But, in order to give you a clear view of their motives in this new trick, and which, I think, is about the last in their budget, I must go back and tell you something of the history of their Debt, and of what are called the Funds. Some years ago the Boroughmongers put me into a loathsome prison for two years, made me pay a thousand pounds fine, and made me enter into recognisances for seven years, only because I expressed my indignation at the flogging of English-men, in the heart of England, under the superintend-ence of hired German troops brought into the country to keep the people in awe. It pleased God, Jack, to preserve my life and health, while I was in that prison. And I employed a part of my time in writing a little book entitled *Paper against Gold*. In this little book I fully explained all the frauds of

Q

what is called the *National Debt*, and of what are called the *Funds*. But as it is possible that you may not have seen that little book, I will here tell you enough about these things to make you see the reasons for the Boroughmongers using this trick of Savings Banks.

The Boroughmongers are, you know, those persons (some Lords, some Baronets, and some Esquires, as they call themselves) who fill, or nominate others to fill, the seats in the House of Commons. *Commons* means the mass of the *people*. So that this is the House of the People, according to the law of the land. The people—you, I, and all of us, ought to vote for the men who sit in this House. But the said Lords, Baronets, and Esquires have taken our rights away, and they nominate the Members themselves. A *monger* is a *dealer*, as ironmonger, cheesemonger, and the like : and as the Lords, Baronets, and Esquires sometimes sell and sometimes buy seats, and as the seats are said to be filled by the people in certain Boroughs, these Lords, Baronets, and Esquires are very properly called *Boroughmongers* ; that is to say, dealers in boroughs or in the seats of boroughs. As all laws and all other matters of government are set up and enforced at the will of the two Houses, against whose will the king cannot stir hand or foot ; and as the Boroughmongers fill the seats of the two Houses, they have all the power, and, of course, the king and the people have none. Being possessed of all the power; being able to tax us at their pleasure; being able to hang us for whatever they please to call a crime; they will, of course, do with our property and persons just what they please. And accordingly, they take from us more than the half of our earnings; and they keep soldiers (whom they deceive) to shoot at us and kill us, if we attempt to resist. They put us in dungeons when they like. And, in Ireland, they compel people to remain shut up in their houses from sunset to sunrise, and if any man, contrary to their commands, goes out of his house in the night, in order to go to the privy, they punish him very severely; and in that unhappy country they transport men and women to Botany Bay without any trial by jury, and merely by the orders of two justices of the peace appointed by themselves.

This, Jack, is horrid work to be going on amongst a people who call themselves *free*; amongst a people who boast of their liberties. But the facts are so; and now I shall explain to you how the Borough-mongers, who are so few in number compared to the whole people, are able to commit these cruel acts and to carry on this abominable tyranny; and you will see that the trick of Savings Banks makes a part of the means, which they now intend to use for the per-petuating of this tyranny.

Formerly, more than a hundred years ago, when

the kings of England had some real power, and before the Boroughmongers took all the powers of king and people into their hands, the people, when the kings behaved amiss, used to rise against them and compel them to act justly. They beheaded Charles the First about one hundred and seventy years ago; and they drove James the Second out of the kingdom; they went so far as to set his family aside for ever, and they put up the present royal family in its stead.

This was all very well; but when King James had been driven out, the Lords and Baronets and Squires conceived the notion of ruling for ever over king and people. They made Parliaments, which used to be annual, three years of duration; and when the members had been elected for three years, the members themselves made a law to make the people obey them for seven years. Thus was the usurpation completed; and from that time to this the Boroughmongers have filled the seats just as it has pleased them to do it; and they have, as I said before, done with our property and our persons just what they have pleased to do.

Now it will naturally be matter of wonder to you, friend Jack, that this small band of persons, and of debauched wretched persons too, any half dozen of whom you would be able to beat with one hand tied down; it will be matter of wonder to you that this contemptible band should have been able thus to subjugate, and hold in bondage so degrading, the whole of the English people. But, Jack, recollect that once a parcel of fat, lazy, drinking, and guttling monks and friars were able to make this same people to work and support them in their laziness and debaucheries, aye, and almost to adore them, too; to go to them, and kneel down and confess their sins to them, and to believe that it was in their power to absolve them of their sins. Now how was it that these fat, these bastard-propagating rascals succeeded in making the people do this? Why by fraud; by deception; by cheatery; by making them believe lies; by frightening them half out of their wits; by making them believe that they would go to hell if they did not work for them. A ten-thousandth part of the people were able to knock the greasy vagabonds on the head; and they would have done it too; but they were afraid of going to hell if they had no priest to pardon them.

Thus did these miscreants govern by fraud. The Boroughmongers, as I shall by and by show, have of late been compelled to resort to open force; but for a long while they governed by fraud alone. First they, by the artful and able agents which they have constantly kept in pay, frightened the people with the pretended dangers of a return of the old king's family. The people were amused with this scarecrow, while the chains were silently forging to bind them with. But the great fraud, the cheat of all cheats, was what they call the national debt. And now, Jack, pray attend to

me; for I am going to explain the chief cause of all
the disgraces and sufferings of the labourers in England; and am also going to explain the reasons or
motives which the Boroughmongers have for setting
on foot this new fraud of Savings Banks.   I beg you,
Jack, if you have no other leisure time, to stay at
home instead of going to church, for one single Sunday.   Shave yourself, put on a clean shirt, and sit
down and read this letter ten times over, until you
understand every word of it.   And if you do that,
you will laugh at the parson and tax-gatherer's coaxings
about Savings Banks.   You will keep your odd pennies
to yourself; or lay them out in bread or bacon.

You have heard, I daresay, a great deal about the
national debt; and now I will tell you what this thing
is, and how it came, and then you will see what an
imposture it is, and how shamefully the people of
England have been duped and robbed.

The Boroughmongers having usurped all the powers
of government, and having begun to pocket the public
money at a great rate, the people grew discontented.
They began to think that they had done wrong in
driving King James away.   In a pretty little fable-book,
there is a fable which says that the frogs, who had a
log of wood for king, prayed to Jupiter to send them
something more active.   He sent them a stork, or
heron, which gobbled them up alive by scores!   The
people of England found in the Boroughmongers

what the poor frogs found in the stork; and they began to cry out against them and to wish for the old king back again.

The Boroughmongers saw their danger, and they adopted measures to prevent it. They saw that if they could make it the interest of a great many rich people to uphold them and their system they should be able to get along. They therefore passed a law to enable themselves to borrow money of rich people; and by the same law they imposed it on the people at large to pay, for ever, the interest of the money so by them borrowed.

The money which they thus borrowed they spent in wars, or divided amongst themselves, in one shape or another. Indeed the money spent in wars was pocketed, for the greater part, by themselves. Thus they owed, in time, immense sums of money; and as they continued to pass laws to compel the nation at large to pay the interest of what they borrowed, spent and pocketed, they called and still call this debt, the debt of the nation; or, in the usual words, the national debt.

It is curious to observe that there has seldom been known in the world any very wicked and mischievous scheme of which a priest of some description or other was not at the bottom. This scheme, certainly as wicked in itself as any that was ever known, and far more mischievous in its consequences than any other, was the offspring of a Bishop of Salisbury, whose name was Burnet; a name that we ought to teach our very children to execrate.   This crafty priest was made a Bishop for his invention of this scheme; a fit reward for such a service.

The Boroughmongers began this debt one hundred and twenty-four years ago.   They have gone on borrowing ever since; and have never paid off one farthing, and never can.   They have continued to pass Acts to make the people pay the interest of what has been borrowed; till, at last, the debt itself amounts to more than all the lands, all the houses, all the trees, all the canals and all the mines would sell for at their full sterling value; and the money to pay the interest is taken out of men's rents and out of their earnings; and you, Jack, as I shall by and by prove to you, pay to the Boroughmongers more than the half of what you receive in weekly wages from your master.

Is not this a pretty state of things?   Pray observe, Jack, the debt far exceeds the real full value of the whole kingdom, if there could be a purchaser found for it.   So that, you see, as to private property no man has any, as long as this debt hangs upon the country. Your master, Farmer Gripe, for instance, calls his farm *his*.   It is none of his, according to the Boroughmongers' law; for that law has pawned it for the payment of the interest of the Boroughmongers' debt; and the pawn must remain as long as the Boroughmongers' law remains. Gripe is compelled to pay out of the yearly value of his farm a certain portion to the debt. He may, indeed, sell the farm ; but he can get only a part of the value ; because the purchaser will have to pay a yearly sum on account of the pawn. In short, the Boroughmongers have, in fact, passed laws to take every man's private property away from him, in whatever portions their debt may demand such taking away ; and a man who thinks himself an owner of land, is at best only a steward who manages it for the Boroughmongers.

This, however, is only a small part of the evil ; for the whole of the rents of the houses and lands and mines and canals would not pay the interest of this debt ; no, and not much more than the half of it. The labour is therefore pawned too. Every man's labour is pawned for the payment of the interest of this debt. Aye, Jack, you may think that you are working for yourself, and that, when on a Saturday night you take nine shillings from Farmer Gripe, the shillings are for your own use. You are grievously deceived, for more than half the sum is paid to the Boroughmongers on account of the pawn. You do not see this, but the fact is so. Come, what are the things in which you expend the nine shillings ? Tea, sugar, tobacco, candles, salt, soap, shoes, beer, bread ; for no meat do you ever taste. On the articles taken together, except bread, you pay far more than half tax ; and you will observe that your master's taxes are, in part, pinched out of you. There is an army employed in Ireland to go with the excisemen and other taxers to make the people pay. If the taxers were to wait at the ale houses and grocers' shops, and receive their portion from your own hands, you would then clearly see that the Boroughmongers take away more than the half of what you earn. You would then clearly see what it is that makes you poor and ragged, and that makes your children cry for the want of a bellyful. You would clearly see that what the hypocrites tell you about this being your lot, and about Providence placing you in such a state in order to try your patience and faith, is all a base falsehood. Why does not Providence place the Boroughmongers and the parsons in a state to try their patience and faith? Is Providence less anxious to save them than to save you? If you could see clearly what you pay on account of the Borough-mongers' pawn, you would see that your misery arises from the designs of a benevolent Providence being counteracted by the measures of the Borough-tyrants.

Your lot, indeed! Your lot assigned by Providence! This is real blasphemy! Just as if Providence, which sends the salt on shore all round our coast, had ordained that you should not have any of it unless you would pay the Boroughmongers fifteen shillings a bushel tax upon it! But what a Providence must that be which would ordain that an Englishman should pay

fifteen shillings tax on a bushel of English salt, while a
Long Islander pays only two shillings and sixpence for
a bushel of the same salt, after it is brought to
America from England? What an idea must we have
of such a Providence as this? Oh no, Jack; this is
not the work of Providence. It is the work of the
Boroughmongers; the pretext about Providence has
been invented to deceive and cheat you, and to perpetuate your slavery.

Well: all is pawned then. The land, the houses,
the canals, the mines, and the labour are pawned for
the payment of the interest of the Boroughmongers
debt. Your labour, mind, Jack, is pawned for the one-
half of its worth. But you will naturally ask, how is
it that the nation, that everybody submits to this?
There's your mistake, Jack. It is not *everybody* that
submits. In the first place there are the Boroughmongers themselves and all their long tribe of relations, legitimate and spurious, who profit from the
taxes, and who have the church livings, which they
enjoy without giving the poor any part of their legal
share of those livings. Then there are all the officers
of army and navy, and all the endless hosts of
place-men and place-women, pensioned men and pensioned women, and all the hosts of tax-gatherers, who
alone, these last I mean, swallow more than would be
necessary to carry on the Government under a reformed
Parliament. But have you forgotten the lenders of

the money which makes the debt? These people live wholly upon the interest of the debt; and of course they approve of your labour, and the labour of every man being pawned. The Boroughmongers have pawned your labour to them. Therefore they like that your labour should be taxed. They cannot be said to submit to the tyranny; they applaud it, and to their utmost they support it.

But you will say, still the mass of the people would, if they had a mind to bestir themselves, be too strong for all these. Very true. But you forget the army, Jack. This is a great military force, armed with bayonets, bullets and cannon-balls, ready at all times and in all places to march or gallop to attack the people, if they attempt to eat sugar or salt without paying the tax. There are forts, under the name of barracks, all over the kingdom, where armed men are kept in readiness for this purpose. In Ireland they actually go in person to help to collect the taxes; and in England they are always ready to do the same Now, suppose, Jack, that a man who has a bit of land by the seaside, were to take up a little of the salt that Providence sends on shore He would be prosecuted. He would resist the process. Soldiers would come and take him away to be tried and *hanged*. Suppose you, Jack, were to dip your rushes into grease, till they came to farthing candles. The Excise would prosecute you. The sheriff would send men to drag you to jail. You would fight in defence of your house and home. You would beat off the sheriff's men. Soldiers would come and kill you, or would take you away to be hanged.

This is the thing by which the Boroughmongers govern. There are enough who would gladly not submit to their tyranny; but there is nobody but themselves who has an army at command.

Nevertheless they are not altogether easy under these circumstances. An army is a two-edged weapon. It may cut the employer as well as the thing that it is employed upon. It is made up of flesh and blood, and of English flesh and blood too. It may not always be willing to move, or to strike when moved. The Boroughmongers see that their titles and estates hang upon the army. They would fain coax the people back again to feelings of reverence and love. They would fain wheedle them into something that shall blunt their hostility. They have been trying Bible-schemes, school-schemes, and soup-schemes. And at last they are trying the Savings Banks scheme, upon which I shall now more particularly address you.

This thing is of the same nature, and its design is the same, as those of the grand scheme of Bishop Burnet. The people are discontented. They feel their oppressions; they seek a change; and some of them have decidedly protested against paying any longer any part of the interest of the debt, which they say ought to be paid, if at all, by those who have borrowed and spent, or pocketed, the money. Now then, in order to enlist great numbers of labourers and artisans on their side, the Boroughmongers have fallen upon the scheme of coaxing them to put small sums into what they call *banks*. These sums they pay large interest upon, and suffer the parties to take them out whenever they please. By this scheme they think to bind great numbers to them and their tyranny. They think that great numbers of labourers and artisans, seeing their little sums increase, as they will imagine, will begin to conceive the hopes of becoming rich by such means; and as these persons are to be told that their money is in the *funds*, they will soon imbibe the spirit of fundholders, and will not care who suffers, or whether freedom or slavery prevail, so that the funds be but safe.

Such is the scheme and such the motives. It will fail of its object, though not unworthy the inventive powers of the servile knaves of Edinburgh. It will fail, first because the men from whom alone the Borough-tyrants have anything to dread, will see through the scheme and despise it; and will, besides, well know that the funds are a mere bubble that may burst, or be bursted at any moment. The parsons appear to be the main tools in this coaxing scheme. They are always at the head of everything which they think likely to support tyranny. The depositors will be domestic servants, particularly women, who will be tickled with the idea of having a fortune in the funds. The Boroughmongers will hint to their tenants that they must get their labourers into the Savings Banks. A preference will be given to such as deposit. The Ladies, the 'Parsons' Ladies,' will scold poor people into the funds. The parish officers will act their part in this compulsory process : and thus will the Boroughmongers get into their hands some millions of the people's money by a sort of 'forced loan': or in other words, a robbery. In order to swell the thing out, the parsons and other tools of the Boroughmongers will lend money in this way themselves, under feigned names ; and we shall, if the system last a year or two, hear boastings of how rich the poor are become.

Now then, Jack, supposing it possible that Farmer Gripe may, under pain of being turned out of your cottage, have made you put your twopence a week into one of these banks, let us see what is the natural consequence of your so doing. Twopence a week is eight shillings and eightpence a year; and the interest will make the amount about nine shillings perhaps. What use is this to you? Will you let it remain ; and will you go on thus for years? You must go on a great many years, indeed, before your deposit amounts to as much as the Boroughmongers take from you in one year! Twopence will buy you a quarter of a pound of meat. This is a dinner for your wife or yourself. You never taste meat. And why are you to give up half a pound of your bread to the Boroughmongers. You are ill; your wife is ill; your children are ill. 'Go to the bank and take out your money,' says the overseer; 'for I'll give you no aid till that be spent.' Thus then, you will have been robbing your own starved belly weekly, to no other end than that of favouring the parish purse, upon which you have a just and legal claim, until the clergy restore to the poor what they have taken from them. As the thing now stands, the poor are starved by others, this scheme is intended to make them assist in the work themselves, at the same time that it binds them to the tyranny.

But, Jack, what a monstrous thing is this, that the Boroughmongers should kindly pass an Act to induce you to save your money, while they take from you five shillings out of every nine that you earn? Why not take less from you! That would be the more natural way to go to work, surely. Why not leave you all your earnings to yourself? Oh, no! They cannot do that. It is from the labour of men like you that the far greater part of the money comes to enrich the Boroughmongers, their relations and dependants.

However, suppose you have gotten together five pounds in a Savings Bank. That is to say in the funds. This is a great deal for you, though it is not half so much as you are compelled to give to the Borough-mongers in one year. This is a great sum. It is much more than you ever will have; but suppose you have it. It is *in the funds*, mind. And now let me tell you what the funds are; which is necessary if you have not read my little book called *Paper against Gold*. The funds is *no place* at all, Jack. It is nothing, Jack, It is moonshine. It is a lie, a bubble, a fraud, a cheat, a humbug. And it is all these in the most perfect degree. People think that the funds is a place where money is kept. They think that it is a place which contains that which they have deposited. But the fact is, that the funds is a word which means nothing that the most of the people think it means. It means the *descriptions of the several sorts of the debt*. Suppose I owed money to a tailor, to a smith, to a shoemaker, to a carpenter, and that I had their several bills in my house. I should in the language of the Borough-mongers, call these bills my *funds*. The Borough-mongers owe some people annuities at three pounds for a hundred; some at four pounds for a hundred; some at five pounds for a hundred; and these annuities, or debts they call their funds. And, Jack, if the Savings Bank people lend them a good parcel of money, they will have that money in these debts or funds. They will be owners of some of those debts which never will and never can be paid.

But what is this money too in which you are to be

paid back again? It is no money. It is paper; and though that paper will pass just at this time; it will not long pass, I can assure you, Jack. When you have worked a fortnight, and get a pound note for it, you set a high value upon the note, because it brings you food. But suppose nobody would take the note from you. Suppose no one would give you anything in exchange for it. You would go back to Farmer Gripe and fling the note in his face. You would insist upon real money, and you would get it, or you would tear down his house. This is what will happen, Jack, in a very short time.

I will explain to you, Jack, how this matter stands. Formerly bank-notes were as good as real money, because anybody that had one might go at any moment, and get real money for it at the Bank. But now the thing is quite changed. The Bank broke some years ago; that is to say, it could not pay its notes in real money; and it never has been able to do it from that time to this; and what is more, it never can do it again. To be sure the paper passes at present. You take it for your work, and others take it of you for bread and tea. But the time may be, and I believe is, very near at hand, when this paper will not pass at all; and then as the Borough-mongers and the Savings Bank people have, and can have, no real money, how are you to get your five pounds back again?

The bank-notes may be all put down at any moment, if any man of talent and resolution choose to put them down; and why may not such a man exist, and have the Disposition to put them down? They are now of value, as I said before, because they will pass; because people will take them and will give victuals and drink for them; but, if nobody would give bread and tea and beer for them, would they then be good for anything? They are taken because people are pretty sure that they can pass them again; but who will take them when he does not think that he can pass them again? And I assure you, Jack, that even I myself could, before next May-day, do that which would prevent any man in England from ever taking a bank-note any more. If you should put five pounds into a Savings Bank, therefore, you could, in such case, never see a farthing in exchange for it.

This being a matter of so much importance to you, I will clearly explain to you how I might easily do the thing. Mind, I do not say that I will do the thing. Indeed, I will not; and I do not know any one that intends to do it. But I will show you how I *might* do it; because it is right that you should know what a ticklish state your poor five pounds will be in if you deposit them in the Savings Bank.

You know, Jack, that *forged* notes pass till people find them out. They keep passing very quietly till they

come to the Bank, and there being known for forged
notes, the man who carries them to the Bank, or
owns them at the time, loses the amount of them.
Suppose now, that Tom were to forge a note, and pay it
to Dick for a pig. Dick would pay it to Bob for some
tea. Bob would send it up to London to pay his tea-
man. The tea-man would send it to the Bank. ₍The
Bank would keep it, and give him nothing for it. If
the tea-man forgot whom he got it from, he must
lose. If he could prove that he got it from
Bob, Bob must lose it; and so on; but either
Dick or Bob or the tea-man must lose it. There
must be a loss somewhere.

Now, it is clear that if there were a great quantity
of forged notes in circulation, people would be afraid to
take notes at all; and that if this great quantity came
out all of a sudden, it would for a while put an end to
all payments and all trade. And if such great quantity
can with safety be put out, I leave you to guess,
Jack, at the situation of your five pounds. I will
now show you, then, that I could do this myself, and
with perfect safety and ease.

I could have made, at a very trifling expense, a
million of pounds in bank-notes of various amounts.
There are fourteen different ways in which I could
send them to England, and lodge them safely there,
without the smallest chance of their arrival being
known to any soul except the man to whom they

should be confided. The Banks might search and ransack every vessel that arrived from America. They might do what they would. They would never detect the cargo !

There they are then, safe in London ; a famous stock of bank-notes, so well executed that no human being except the Bank people would be able to discover the counterfeit. The agent takes a parcel at a time, and drops them in the street in the dark. This work he carries on for a week or two in such streets as are best calculated for the purpose, till he has well stocked the town. He may do the same at Portsmouth and other great towns if he please, and he may send off large supplies by post.

Now, Jack, suppose you were up at London with your master's waggon. You might find a parcel of notes. You would go to the first shop to buy your wife a gown and your children some clothes, yourself a hat, a greatcoat, and some shoes. The rest you would lay out at shops on the road home ; for the sooner you got rid of this *foundal*, the less chance of having it taken from you. The shopkeepers would thank you for your custom, and your wife's heart would bound with joy.

The notes would travel about most merrily. At last they would come to the Bank. The holders would lose them ; but you would gain by them. So that, upon the whole, there would be no loss, and the maker of the notes would have no gain. Others would find, and nearly all would do like you. In a few days the notes would find their way to the Bank in great numbers, where they would all be stopped. The news would spread abroad. The thieftakers would be busy. Every man who had had his note stopped at the Bank would alarm his neighbourhood. The country would ring with the news. Nobody would take a bank-note. All business would be at a stand. The farmers would sell no corn for bank-notes. The millers would have nothing else to pay with. No markets, because no money. The baker would be able to get no flour. He could sell no bread, for nobody would have money to pay him.

Jack, this thing will assuredly take place. Mind, I tell you so. I have been right in my predictions on former occasions; and I am not wrong now. I beg you to believe me; or, at any rate, to blame yourself if you lose by such an event. In the midst of this hubbub what will you do? Farmer Gripe will, I daresay, give you something to eat for your labour. But what will become of your five pounds? That sum you have in the Savings Bank, and as you are to have it out at any time when you please, your wife sets off to draw it. The banker gives her a five-pound note. She brings it; but nobody will take it of you for a pig, for bread, for clothing, or for anything else! And this, Jack, will be the fate of all those who shall be weak enough to put their money into those banks !

I beg you, Jack, not to rely on the power of the Boroughmongers in this case. Anything that is to be done with halters, gags, dungeons, bayonets, powder, or ball, they can do a great deal at; but they are not conjurers; they are not wizards. They cannot prevent a man from dropping bank-notes in the dark; and they cannot make people believe in the goodness of that which they must know to be bad. If they could hold a sword to every man's breast, they might indeed do something; but short of this, nothing that they can do would be of any avail. However, the truth is that they, in such case, will have no sword at all. An army is a powerful weapon; but an army must be paid. Soldiers have been called machines; but they are eating and drinking machines. With good food and drink they will go far and do much; but without them, they will not stir an inch. And in such a case whence is to come the money to pay them? In short, Jack, the Boroughmongers would drop down dead, like men in an apoplexy, and you would, as soon as things got to rights, have your bread and beer and meat and everything in abundance.

The Boroughmongers possess no means of preventing the complete success of the dropping plan. If they do, they ought to thank me for giving them a warning of their danger; and for telling them that if they do prevent the success of such a plan, they are the cleverest fellows in this world.

I now, Jack, take my leave of you, hoping that you will not be coaxed out of your money, and assuring you that I am your friend,

WM. COBBETT.

VII.—'THE LETTERS OF MALACHI MALAGROWTHER'

By Sir Walter Scott

(*To what has been said in the Introduction respecting the* Letters of Malachi Malagrowther *it is only necessary to add that their immediate cause was a Bill due to the very commercial crisis which indirectly ruined Scott himself, and introduced in the spring of* 1826 *for stopping the note circulation of private banks altogether, while limiting that of the Bank of England to notes of £5 and upwards. The scheme, which was to extend to the whole of Great Britain, was from the first unpopular in Scotland, and Scott plunged into the fray. The letters excited or coincided with such violent opposition throughout the country that the Bill was limited to England only. As Scott was a strong Tory, his friends in the Government, especially Lord Melville and Croker (who was officially employed to answer* 'Malachi'), *were rather sore at his action.*

*He defended himself in some spirited private letters,
which will be found in Lockhart.*)

A Letter on the Proposed Change of Currency

To the Editor of the Edinburgh Weekly Journal

My dear Mr. Journalist—I am by pedigree a
discontented person, so that you may throw this letter
into the fire, if you have any apprehensions of incurring the displeasure of your superiors. I am, in
fact, the lineal descendant of Sir Mungo Malagrowther,
who makes a figure in the *Fortunes of Nigel*, and have
retained a reasonable proportion of his ill-luck, and,
in consequence, of his ill-temper. If, therefore, I
should chance to appear too warm and poignant in
my observations, you must impute it to the hasty and
peevish humour which I derive from my ancestor.
But, at the same time, it often happens that this disposition leads me to speak useful, though unpleasant
truths, when more prudent men hold their tongues
and eat their pudding. A lizard is an ugly and dis-
gusting thing enough ; but, methinks, if a lizard were
to run over my face and awaken me, which is said to
be their custom when they observe a snake approach a
sleeping person, I should neither scorn his intimation,

nor feel justifiable in crushing him to death, merely because he is a filthy little abridgment of a crocodile. Therefore, 'for my love, I pray you, wrong me not.'

I am old, sir, poor, and peevish, and therefore I may be wrong; but when I look back on the last fifteen or twenty years, and more especially on the last ten, I think I see my native country of Scotland, if it is yet to be called by a title so discriminative, falling, so far as its national, or rather, perhaps, I ought now to say its *provincial*, interests are concerned, daily into more absolute contempt. Our ancestors were a people of some consideration in the councils of the empire. So late as my own younger days, an English minister would have paused, even in a favourite measure, if a reclamation of national rights had been made by a member for Scotland, supported as it uniformly then was, by the voice of her representatives and her people. Such ameliorations in our peculiar system as were thought necessary, in order that North Britain might keep pace with her sister in the advance of improvement, were suggested by our own countrymen, persons well acquainted with our peculiar system of laws (as different from those of England as from those of France), and who knew exactly how to adapt the desired alteration to the principle of our legislative enactments, so that the whole machine might, as mechanics say, work well

and easily.   For a long time this wholesome check
upon innovation, which requires the assimilation of a
proposed improvement with the general constitution of
the country to which it has been recommended, and
which ensures that important point, by stipulating that
the measure shall originate with those to whom the
spirit of the constitution is familiar, has been, so far as
Scotland is concerned, considerably disused.   Those
who have stepped forward to repair the gradual
failure of our constitutional system of law, have been
persons that, howsoever qualified in other respects,
have had little further knowledge of its construction
than could be acquired by a hasty and partial survey,
taken just before they commenced their labours.   Scotland and her laws have been too often subjected to
the alterations of any person who chose to found himself a reputation, by bringing in a bill to cure some
defect which had never been felt in practice, but
which was represented as a frightful bugbear to
English statesmen, who, wisely and judiciously tenacious of the legal practice and principles received at
home, are proportionally startled at the idea of anything abroad which cannot be brought to assimilate
with them.

The English seem to have made a compromise
with the active tendency to innovation, which is one
great characteristic of the day.   Wise and sagacious
themselves, they are nervously jealous of innovations

in their own laws—*Nolumus leges Angliae mutari*, is written on the skirts of their judicial robes, as the most sacred texts of Scripture were inscribed on the phylacteries of the Rabbis. The belief that the Common Law of England constitutes the perfection of human reason, is a maxim bound upon their foreheads. Law Monks they have been called in other respects, and like monks they are devoted to their own Rule, and admit no question of its infallibility. There can be no doubt that their love of a system, which, if not perfect, has so much in it that is excellent, originates in the most praiseworthy feelings. Call it if you will the prejudice of education, it is still a prejudice honourable in itself, and useful to the public. I only find fault with it, because, like the Friars in the Duenna monopolising the bottle, these English monks will not tolerate in their lay brethren of the north the slightest pretence to a similar feeling.

In England, therefore, no innovation can be proposed affecting the administration of justice, without being subjected to the strict enquiry of the Guardians of the Law, and afterwards resisted pertinaciously, until time and the most mature and reiterated discussion shall have proved its utility, nay, its necessity. The old saying is still true in all its points—Touch but a cobweb in Westminster Hall, and the old spider will come out in defence of it. This caution may sometimes postpone the adoption of useful amendments, but it operates to prevent all hasty and experimental innovations; and it is surely better that existing evils should be endured for some time longer, than that violent remedies should be hastily adopted, the unforeseen and unprovided for consequences of which are often so much more extensive than those which had been foreseen and reckoned upon. An ordinary mason can calculate upon the exact gap which will be made by the removal of a corner stone in an old building; but what architect, not intimately acquainted with the whole edifice, can presume even to guess how much of the structure is, or is not, to follow?

The English policy in this respect is a wise one, and we have only to wish they would not insist in keeping it all to themselves. But those who are most devoted to their own religion have least sympathy for the feelings of dissenters; and a spirit of proselytism has of late shown itself in England for extending the benefits of their system, in all its strength and weakness, to a country which has been hitherto flourishing and contented under its own. They adopted the conclusion that all English enactments are right; but the system of municipal law in Scotland is not English, therefore it is wrong. Under sanction of this syllogism, our rulers have indulged and encouraged a spirit of experiment and innovation at our expense, which they resist obstinately when it is to be carried through at their own risk.

For more than half of last century, this was a practice not to be thought of. Scotland was during that period disaffected, in bad humour, armed too, and smarting under various irritating recollections. This is not the sort of patient for whom an experimental legislator chooses to prescribe. There was little chance of making Saunders take the patent pill by persuasion—main force was a dangerous argument, and some thought claymores had edges.

This period passed away, a happier one arrived, and Scotland, no longer the object of terror, or at least great uneasiness, to the British Government, was left from the year 1750 under the guardianship of her own institutions, to win her silent way to national wealth and consequence. Contempt probably procured for her the freedom from interference, which had formerly been granted out of fear; for the medical faculty are as slack in attending the garrets of paupers as the caverns of robbers. But neglected as she was, and perhaps *because* she was neglected, Scotland, reckoning her progress during the space from the close of the American War to the present day, has increased her prosperity in a ratio more than five times greater than that of her more fortunate and richer sister. She is now worth the attention of the learned faculty, and God knows she has had plenty of it. She has been bled and purged, spring and fall, and *talked* into courses of physic, for which she had little occasion. She has been of late a sort of experimental farm, upon which every political student has been permitted to try his theory—a kind of common property, where every juvenile statesman has been encouraged to make his inroads, as in Moray land, where, anciently, according to the idea of the old Highlanders, all men had a right to take their prey—a subject in a common dissecting room, left to the scalpel of the junior students, with the degrading inscription,—*fiat experimentum in corpore vili.*

I do not mean to dispute, Sir, that much alteration was necessary in our laws, and that much benefit has followed many of the great changes which have taken place. I do not mean to deprecate a gradual approach to the English system, especially in commercial law. The Jury Court, for example, was a fair experiment, in my opinion, cautiously introduced as such, and placed under such regulations as might best assimilate its forms with those of the existing Supreme Court. I beg, therefore, to be considered as not speaking of the alterations themselves, but of the apparent hostility towards our municipal institutions, as repeatedly manifested in the course of late proceedings, tending to force and wrench them into a similarity with those of England.

The opinions of our own lawyers, nay, of our

Judges, than whom wiser and more honourable men never held that character, have been, if report speaks true, something too much neglected and controlled in the course of these important changes, in which, methinks, they ought to have had a leading and primary voice. They have been almost avowedly regarded not as persons the best qualified to judge of proposed innovations, but as prejudiced men, determined to oppose them, right or wrong. The last public Commission was framed on the very principle, that if Scotch lawyers were needs to be employed, a sufficient number of these should consist of gentlemen, who, whatever their talents and respectability might be in other respects, had been too long estranged from the study of Scottish law to retain any accurate recollection of an abstruse science, or any decided partiality for its technical forms. This was done avowedly for the purpose of evading the natural partiality of the Scottish Judges and practitioners to their own system ; that partiality which the English themselves hold so sacred a feeling in their own Judges and Counsel learned in the law. I am not, I repeat, complaining of the result of the Commissions, but of the spirit in which the alterations were undertaken. Unquestionably much was done in brushing up and improving the old machinery of Scottish Law Courts, and in making it move more rapidly, though scarce, I think, more correctly than before. Dispatch has

s

been much attended to. But it may be ultimately found that the timepiece which runs fastest does not intimate the hour most accurately. At all events, the changes have been made and established—there let them rest. And had I, Malachi Malagrowther, the sole power to-morrow of doing so, I would not restore the old forms of judicial proceedings; because I hold the constitution of Courts of Justice too serious matters to be put back or forward at pleasure, like a boy's first watch, merely for experiment's sake.

What I *do* complain of is the general spirit of slight and dislike manifested to our national establishments by those of the sister country who are so very zealous in defending their own; and not less do I complain of their jealousy of the opinions of those who cannot but be much better acquainted than they, both with the merits and deficiencies of the system, which hasty and imperfectly informed judges have shown themselves so anxious to revolutionise.

There is no explanation to be given of this but one—namely, the entire conviction and belief of our English brethren that the true Themis is worshipped in Westminster Hall, and that her adorers cannot be too zealous in her service; while she, whose image an ingenious artist has depicted balancing herself upon a *tee-totum* on the southern window of the Parliament House of Edinburgh, is a mere idol,—a Diana of Ephesus,—whom her votaries worship, either because

her shrine brings great gain to the craftsmen, or out
of an ignorant and dotard superstition, which induces
them to prefer the old Scottish *Mumpsimus* to the
modern English *Sumpsimus*. Now, this is not fair
construction in our friends, whose intentions in our
behalf, we allow, are excellent, but who certainly are
scarcely entitled to beg the question at issue without
inquiry or discussion, or to treat us as the Spaniards
treated the Indians, whom they massacred for wor-
shipping the image of the Sun, while they themselves
bowed down to that of the Virgin Mary. Even Queen
Elizabeth was contented with the evasive answer of
Melville, when hard pressed with the trying question,
whether Queen Mary or she were the fairest. We are
willing, in the spirit of that answer, to say that the
Themis of Westminster Hall is the best fitted to pre-
side over the administration of the larger, and more
fertile country of beef and pudding; while she of the
tee-totum (placed in that precarious position, we presume, to express her instability, since these new lights
were struck out) claims a more limited but equally
respectful homage, within her ancient jurisdiction—
sua paupera regna—the Land of Cakes. If this
compromise does not appease the ardour of our
brethren for converting us to English forms and
fashions, we must use the scriptural question, "Who
hath required these things at your hands?"

The inquiries and result of another Commission

are too much to the purpose to be suppressed.   The
object was to investigate the conduct of the Revenue
Boards in Ireland and Scotland.   In the former, it is
well known, great mismanagement was discovered; for
Pat, poor fellow, had been playing the loon to a considerable extent.   In Scotland, *not a shadow of abuse
prevailed*.   You would have thought, Mr. Journalist,
that the Irish Boards would have been reformed in
some shape, and the Scotch Establishments honourably
acquitted, and suffered to continue on the footing of
independence which they had so long enjoyed, and
of which they had proved themselves so worthy.   Not
so, sir.   The Revenue Boards, in both countries, under-
went exactly the same regulation, were deprived of
their independent consequence, and placed under
the superintendence of English control ; the innocent
and the guilty being treated in every respect alike.
Now, on the side of Scotland, this was like Trinculo
losing his bottle in the pool—there was not only dishonour in the thing, but an infinite loss.

I have heard two reasons suggested for this indis-
criminating application of punishment to the innocent
and to the culpable.

In the first place, it was honestly confessed that
Ireland would never have quietly submitted to the in-
dignity offered to her, unless poor inoffensive Scotland
had been included in the regulation.   The Green Isle,
it seems, was of the mind of a celebrated lady of quality,

who, being about to have a decayed tooth drawn, refused to submit to the operation till she had seen the dentist extract a sound and serviceable grinder from the jaws of her waiting-woman—and her humour was to be gratified. The lady was a termagant dame —the wench a tame-spirited simpleton—the dentist an obliging operator—and the teeth of both were drawn accordingly.

This gratification of his humours is gained by Pat's being up with the pike and shillelagh on any or no occasion. God forbid Scotland should retrograde towards such a state—much better that the Deil, as in Burns's song, danced away with the whole excisemen in the country. We do not want to hear her prate of her number of millions of men, and her old military exploits. We had better remain in union with England, even at the risk of becoming a subordinate species of Northumberland, as far as national consequence is concerned, than remedy ourselves by even hinting the possibility of a rupture. But there is no harm in wishing Scotland to have just so much ill-nature, according to her own proverb, as may keep her good-nature from being abused; so much national spirit as may determine her to stand by her own rights, conducting her assertion of them with every feeling of respect and amity toward England.

The other reason alleged for this equal distribution of *punishment*, as if it had been the influence of the common sun, or the general rain, to the just and the unjust, was one which is extremely predominant at present with our Ministers—the *necessity* of *Uniformity* in all such cases ; and the consideration what an awkward thing it would be to have a Board of Excise or Customs remaining independent in the one country, solely because they had, without impeachment, discharged their duty; while the same establishment was cashiered in another, for no better reason than that it had been misused.

This reminds us of an incident, said to have befallen at the Castle of Glammis, when these venerable towers were inhabited by a certain old Earl of Strathmore, who was as great an admirer of uniformity as the Chancellor of the Exchequer could have desired. He and his gardener directed all in the garden and pleasure grounds upon the ancient principle of exact correspondence between the different parts, so that each alley had its brother; a principle which, renounced by gardeners, is now adopted by statesmen. It chanced once upon a time that a fellow was caught committing some petty theft, and, being taken in the manner, was sentenced by the Bailie Macwheeble of the jurisdiction to stand for a certain time in the baronial pillory, called the *jougs*, being a collar and chain, one of which contrivances was attached to each side of the portal of the great avenue which led to the castle.   The thief was turned over accordingly to the gardener, as ground-officer, to see the punishment duly inflicted. When the Thane of Glammis returned from his morning ride, he was surprised to find both sides of the gateway accommodated each with a prisoner, like a pair of heraldic supporters, *chained* and *collared proper*. He asked the gardener, whom he found watching the place of punishment, as his duty required, whether another delinquent had been detected? " No, my Lord," said the gardener, in the tone of a man excellently well satisfied with himself,—" but I thought the single fellow looked very awkward standing on one side of the gateway, so I gave half a crown to one of the labourers to stand on the other side for *uniformity's sake*." This is exactly a case in point, and probably the only one which can be found—with this sole difference, that I do not hear that the members of the Scottish Revenue Board got any boon for standing in the pillory with those of Ireland—for uniformity's sake.

Lastly, sir, I come to this business of extending the provisions of the Bill prohibiting the issue of notes under five pounds to Scotland, in six months after the period that the regulation shall be adopted in England.

I am not about to enter upon the question which so much agitates speculative writers upon the wealth of nations, or attempt to discuss what proportion of the precious metals ought to be detained within a country; what are the best means of keeping it there; or to what extent the want of specie can be supplied by paper credit : I will not ask if a poor man can be made a rich one, by compelling him to buy a service of plate, instead of the delf ware which served his turn. These are questions I am not adequate to solve. But I beg leave to consider the question in a practical point of view, and to refer myself entirely to experience.

I assume, without much hazard of contradiction, that Banks have existed in Scotland for near one hundred and twenty years—that they have flourished, and the country has flourished with them—and that during the last fifty years particularly, provincial Banks, or branches of the principal established and chartered Banks, have gradually extended themselves in almost every Lowland district in Scotland ; that the notes, and especially the small notes, which they distribute, entirely supply the demand for a medium of currency; and that the system has so completely expelled gold from the country of Scotland, that you never by any chance espy a guinea there, unless in the purse of an accidental stranger, or in the coffers of these Banks themselves. This is granting the facts of the case as broadly as can be asked.

It is not less unquestionable that the consequence of this Banking system, as conducted in Scotland, has been attended with the greatest advantage to the country. The facility which it has afforded to the industrious and enterprising agriculturalist or manufacturer, as well as to the trustees of the public in executing national works, has converted Scotland from a poor, miserable, and barren country, into one, where, if nature has done less, art and industry have done more, than in perhaps any country in Europe, England herself not excepted. Through means of the credit which this system has afforded, roads have been made, bridges built, and canals dug, opening up to reciprocal communication the most sequestered districts of the country—manufactures have been established, unequalled in extent or success—wastes have been converted into productive farms—the productions of the earth for human use have been multiplied twentyfold, while the wealth of the rich and the comforts of the poor have been extended in the same proportion. And all this in a country where the rigour of the climate, and sterility of the soil, seem united to set improvement at defiance. Let those who remember Scotland forty years since, bear witness if I speak truth or falsehood.

There is no doubt that this change has been produced by the facilities of procuring credit, which the Scottish Banks held forth, both by discounting bills, and by granting cash-accounts. Every undertaking of consequence, whether by the public or by individuals, has been carried on by such means; at least exceptions are extremely rare.

There is as little doubt that the Banks could not have furnished these necessary funds of cash, without enjoying the reciprocal advantage of their own notes being circulated in consequence, and by means of the accommodation thus afforded. It is not to be expected that every undertaking which the system enabled speculators or adventurers to commence, should be well-judged, attentively carried on, or successful in issue. Imprudence in some cases, misfortune in others, have had their usual quantity of victims. But in Scotland, as elsewhere, it has happened in many instances that improvements, which turned out ruinous to those who undertook them, have, notwithstanding, themselves ultimately produced the most beneficial advantages to the country, which derived in such instances an addition to its general prosperity, even from the undertakings which had proved destructive to the private fortune of the projectors.

Not only did the Banks dispersed throughout Scotland afford the means of bringing the country to an unexpected and almost marvellous degree of prosperity, but in no considerable instance, save one, have their own over-speculating undertakings been the means of interrupting that prosperity. The solitary exception was the undertaking called the Ayr Bank, rashly entered into by a large body of country gentlemen and others, unacquainted with commercial affairs, and who had moreover the misfortune not only to set out on false principles, but to get false rogues for their principal agents and managers. The fall of this Bank brought much calamity on the country; but two things are remarkable in its history : First, that under its too prodigal, yet beneficial influence, a fine county (that of Ayr) was converted from a desert into a fertile land. Secondly, that, though at a distant interval, the Ayr Bank paid all its engagements, and the loss only fell on the original stockholders. The warning was, however, a terrible one, and has been so well attended to in Scotland, that very few attempts seem to have been afterwards made to establish Banks prematurely—that is, where the particular district was not in such an advanced state as to require the support of additional credit; for in every such case, it was judiciously foreseen, the forcing a capital on the district could only lead to wild speculation, instead of supporting solid and promising undertakings.

The character and condition of the persons pursuing the profession ought to be noticed, however slightly. The Bankers of Scotland have been, generally speaking, *good* men, in the mercantile phrase, showing, by the wealth of which they have died possessed, that their credit was sound ; and *good* men also, many of them eminently so, in the more extensive and better sense of the word, manifesting, by the excellence of their character, the fairness of the means by which their riches were acquired. There may have been, among so numerous a body, men of a different character, fishers in troubled waters, capitalists who sought gain not by the encouragement of fair trade and honest industry, but by affording temporary fuel to rashness or avarice. But the number of upright traders in the profession has narrowed the means of mischief which such Christian Shylocks would otherwise have possessed. There was loss, there was discredit, in having recourse to such characters, when honest wants could be fairly supplied by upright men, and on liberal terms. Such reptiles have been confined in Scotland to batten upon their proper prey of folly, and feast, like worms, on the corruption in which they are bred.

Since the period of the Ayr Bank, now near half a century, I recollect very few instances of Banking Companies issuing notes which have become insolvent. One, about thirty years since, was the Merchant Bank of Stirling, which never was in high credit, having been known almost at the time of its commencement by the odious nickname of *Black in the West*. Another was within these ten years, the East Lothian Banking Company, whose affairs had been very ill conducted by a villainous manager. In both cases, the notes were paid up in full. In the latter case, they were taken up by one of the most respectable houses in Edinburgh; so that all current engagements were paid without the least check to the circulation of their notes, or inconvenience to poor or rich, who happened to have them in possession. The Union Bank of Falkirk also became insolvent within these fifteen years, but paid up its engagements without much loss to the creditors. Other cases there may have occurred, not coming within my recollection ; but I think none which made any great sensation, or could at all affect the general confidence of the country in the stability of the system. None of these bankruptcies excited much attention, or, as we have seen, caused any considerable loss.

In the present unhappy commercial distress, I have always heard and understood that the Scottish Banks have done all in their power to alleviate the evils which came thickening on the country ; and far from acting illiberally, that they have come forward to support the tottering credit of the commercial world with a frankness which augured the most perfect confidence in their own resources. We have heard of only one provincial Bank being even for a moment in the predicament of suspicion ; and of that copartnery the funds and credit were so well understood, that their correspondents in Edinburgh, as in the case of the East Lothian Bank formerly mentioned, at once guaranteed the payment of their notes, and saved the public even from momentary agitation, and individuals from the possibility of distress. I ask what must be the stability of a system of credit of which such an universal earthquake could not displace or shake even the slightest individual portion ?

Thus stands the case in Scotland; and it is clear any restrictive enactment affecting the Banking system, or their mode of issuing notes, must be adopted in consequence of evils, operating elsewhere perhaps, but certainly unknown in this country.

In England, unfortunately, things have been very different, and the insolvency of many provincial Banking Companies, of the most established reputation for stability, has greatly distressed the country, and alarmed London itself, from the necessary reaction of their misfortunes upon their correspondents in the capital.

I do not think, sir, that the advocate of Scotland is called upon to go further, in order to plead an exemption from any experiment which England may think proper to try to cure her own malady, than to say such malady does not exist in her jurisdiction. It is surely enough to plead, 'We are well, our pulse and complexion prove it—let those who are sick take physic.' But the opinion of the English Ministers is widely different; for, granting our premisses, they deny our conclusion.

The peculiar humour of a friend, whom I lost some years ago, is the only one I recollect, which jumps precisely with the reasoning of the Chancellor of the Exchequer. My friend was an old Scottish laird, a bachelor and a humorist—wealthy, convivial, and hospitable, and of course having always plenty of company about him.   He had a regular custom of swallowing every night in the world one of Dr. Anderson's pills, for which reasons may be readily imagined.   But it is not so easy to account for his insisting on every one of his guests taking the same medicine, and whether it was by way of patronising the medicine, which is in some sense a national receipt, or whether the mischievous old wag amused himself with anticipating the scenes of delicate embarrassment, which the dispensation sometimes produced in the course of the night, I really cannot even guess.   What is equally strange, he pressed the request with a sort of eloquence which succeeded with every guest.   No man escaped, though there were few who did not make resistance.   His powers of persuasion would have been invaluable to a minister of state.   'What! not one *Leetle Anderson*, to oblige your friend, your host, your entertainer!   He had taken one himself—he would take another, if you pleased—surely what was good for his complaint must of course be beneficial to yours?' It was in vain you pleaded your being perfectly well,— your detesting the medicine,—your being certain it would not agree with you—none of the apologies were received as valid.   You might be warm, pathetic or sulky, fretful or patient, grave or serious in testifying your repugnance, but you were equally a doomed man; escape was impossible.   Your host was in his turn eloquent,—authoritative,—facetious,—argumentative,

—precatory,—pathetic, above all, pertinacious. No guest was known to escape the *Leetle Anderson*. The last time I experienced the laird's hospitality there were present at the evening meal the following catalogue of guests :—a Bond-street dandy, of the most brilliant water, drawn thither by the temptation of grouse-shooting—a writer from the neighbouring borough (the lairds *doer*, I believe),—two country lairds, men of reserved and stiff habits—three sheep-farmers, as stiff-necked and stubborn as their own haltered rams—and I, Malachi Malagrowther, not facile or obvious to persuasion. There was also the Esculapius of the vicinity—one who gave, but elsewhere was never known to *take* medicine. All succumbed—each took, after various degrees of resistance according to his peculiar fashion, his own *Leetle Anderson*. The doer took a brace. On the event I am silent. None had reason to congratulate himself on his complaisance. The laird has slept with his ancestors for some years, remembered sometimes with a smile on account of his humorous eccentricities, always with a sigh when his surviving friends and neighbours reflect on his kindliness and genuine beneficence. I have only to add that I hope he has not bequeathed to the Chancellor of the Exchequer, otherwise so highly gifted, his invincible powers of persuading folks to take medicine, which their constitutions do not require.

Have I argued my case too high in supposing that

the present intended legislative enactment is as inapplicable to Scotland as a pair of elaborate knee-buckles would be to the dress of a kilted Highlander? I think not.

I understand Lord Liverpool and the Chancellor of the Exchequer distinctly to have admitted the fact, that no distress whatever had originated in Scotland from the present issuing of small notes of the bankers established there, whether provincial in the strict sense, or sent abroad by branches of the larger establishments settled in the metropolis. No proof can be desired better than the admission of the adversary.

Nevertheless, we have been positively informed by the newspapers that Ministers see no reason why any law adopted on this subject should not be imperative over all his Majesty's dominions, including Scotland, *for uniformity's sake.* In my opinion they might as well make a law that the Scotsman, for uniformity's sake, should not eat oatmeal, because it is found to give Englishmen the heartburn. If an ordinance prohibiting the oatcake, can be accompanied with a regulation capable of being enforced, that in future, for uniformity's sake, our moors and uplands shall henceforth bear the purest wheat, I for one have no objection to the regulation. But till Ben Nevis be level with Norfolkshire, though the natural wants of the two nations may be the same, the extent of these wants, natural or commercial, and the mode of supplying

T

them, must be widely different, let the rule of uniformity be as absolute as it will.   The nation which cannot raise wheat, must be allowed to eat oat-bread ; the nation which is too poor to retain a circulating medium of the precious metals, must be permitted to supply its place with paper credit ; otherwise, they must go without food, and without currency.

If I were called on, Mr. Journalist, I think I could give some reasons why the system of banking which has been found well adapted for Scotland is not proper for England, and why there is no reason for inflicting upon us the intended remedy ; in other words, why this political balsam of Fierabras which is to relieve Don Quixote, may have a great chance to poison Sancho.   With this view, I will mention briefly some strong points of distinction affecting the comparative credit of the banks in England and in Scotland ; and they seem to furnish, to one inexperienced in political economies (upon the transcendental doctrines of which so much stress is now laid), very satisfactory reasons for the difference which is not denied to exist bewixt the effects of the same general system in different countries.

In Scotland, almost all Banking Companies consist of a considerable number of persons, many of them men of landed property, whose landed estates, with the burthens legally affecting them, may be learned from the records, for the expense of a few shillings ; so that all the world knows, or may know, the general basis on which their credit rests, and the extent of real property, which, independent of their personal means, is responsible for their commercial engagements. In most banking establishments this fund of credit is considerable, in others immense; especially in those where the shares are numerous, and are held in small proportions, many of them by persons of landed estates, whose fortunes, however large, and however small their share of stock, must all be liable to the engagements of the Bank. In England, as I believe, the number of the partners engaged in a banking concern cannot exceed five; and though of late years their landed property has been declared subject to be attacked by their commercial creditors, yet no one can learn, without incalculable trouble, the real value of that land, or with what mortgages it is burthened. Thus, *cæteris paribus*, the English banker cannot make his solvency manifest to the public, therefore cannot expect, or receive, the same unlimited trust, which is willingly and securely reposed in those of the same profession in Scotland.

Secondly, the circulation of the Scottish bank-notes is free and unlimited; an advantage arising from their superior degree of credit. They pass without a shadow of objection through the whole limits of Scotland, and, though they cannot be legally tendered, are current nearly as far as York in England. Those of English Banking Companies seldom extend beyond a very limited horizon : in two or three stages from the place where they are issued, many of them are objected to, and give perpetual trouble to any traveller who has happened to take them in change on the road.   Even the most creditable provincial notes never approach London in a free tide—never circulate like blood to the heart, and from thence to the extremities, but are current within a limited circle ; often, indeed, so very limited, that the notes issued in the morning, to use an old simile, fly out like pigeons from the dovecot, and are sure to return in the evening to the spot which they have left at break of day.

Owing to these causes, and others which I forbear mentioning, the profession of provincial Bankers in England is limited in its regular profits, and uncertain in its returns, to a degree unknown in Scotland ; and is, therefore, more apt to be adopted in the South by men of sanguine hopes and bold adventure (both frequently disproportioned to the extent of their capital), who sink in mines or other hazardous speculations the funds which their banking credit enables them to command, and deluge the country with notes, which, on some unhappy morning, are found not worth a penny—as those to whom the foul fiend has given apparent treasures are said in due time to discover they are only pieces of slate.

I am aware it may be urged that the restrictions imposed on those English provincial Banks are necessary to secure the supremacy of the Bank of England; on the same principle on which dogs, kept near the purlieus of a royal forest, were anciently lamed by the cutting off of one of the claws, to prevent their interfering with the royal sport. This is a very good regulation for England, for what I know; but why should the Scottish institutions, which do not, and cannot interfere with the influence of the Bank of England, be put on a level with those of which such jealousy is, justly or unjustly, entertained? We receive no benefit from that immense establishment, which, like a great oak, overshadows England from Tweed to Cornwall. Why should our national plantations be cut down or cramped for the sake of what affords us neither shade nor shelter, and which, besides, can take no advantage by the injury done to us? Why should we be subjected to a monopoly from which we derive no national benefit?

I have only to add that Scotland has not felt the slightest inconvenience from the want of specie, nay, that it has never been in request among them. A tradesman will take a guinea more unwillingly than a note of the same value—to the peasant the coin is unknown. No one ever wishes for specie save when upon a journey to England. In occasional runs upon particular houses, the notes of other Banking Companies have always been the value asked for—no holder of these notes ever demanded specie. The

credit of one establishment might be doubted for
the time—that of the general system was never
brought into question. Even avarice, the most
suspicious of passions, has in no instance I ever heard
of, desired to compose her hoards by an accumulation
of the precious metals. The confidence in the credit
of our ordinary medium has not been doubted even
in the dreams of the most irritable and jealous of
human passions.

All these considerations are so obvious that a
statesman so acute as Mr. Robinson must have taken
them in at the first glance, and must at the same
time have deemed them of no weight, compared with
the necessary conformity between the laws of the two
kingdoms. I must, therefore, speak to the justice of
this point of uniformity.

Sir, my respected ancestor, Sir Mungo, when he
had the distinguished honour to be *whipping*, or
rather *whipped boy*, to his Majesty King James the
Sixth of gracious memory, was always, in virtue of his
office, scourged when the king deserved flogging;
and the same equitable rule seems to distinguish the
conduct of Government towards Scotland, as one of
the three United Kingdoms. If Pat is guilty of pecu-
lation, Sister Peg loses her Boards of Revenue—if
John Bull's cashiers mismanage his money-matters,
those who have conducted Sister Margaret's to their
own great honour, and her no less advantage, must

be deprived of the power of serving her in future ; at least that power must be greatly restricted and limited.

'Quidquid delirant reges plectuntur Achivi.'

That is to say, if our superiors of England and Ireland eat sour grapes, the Scottish teeth must be set on edge as well as their own. An uniformity in benefits may be well—an uniformity in penal measures, towards the innocent and the guilty, in prohibitory regulations, whether necessary or not, seems harsh law, and worse justice.

This levelling system, not equitable in itself, is infinitely unjust, if a story, often told by my poor old grandfather, was true, which I own I am inclined to doubt. The old man, sir, had learned in his youth, or dreamed in his dotage, that Scotland had become an integral part of England,—not in right of conquest, or rendition, or through any right of inheritance—but in virtue of a solemn Treaty of Union. Nay, so distinct an idea had he of this supposed Treaty, that he used to recite one of its articles to this effect :—
'That the laws in use within the kingdom of Scotland, do, after the Union, remain in the same force as before, but alterable by the Parliament of Great Britain, with this difference between the laws concerning public right, policy, and civil government, and those which concern private right, that the former may be made the same through the whole

United Kingdom ; but that no alteration be made on laws which concern private right, *excepting for the evident utility of the subjects within Scotland.'* When the old gentleman came to the passage, which you will mark in italics, he always clenched his fist, and exclaimed, 'Nemo me impune lacessit!' which, I presume, are words belonging to the black art, since there is no one in the Modern Athens conjuror enough to understand their meaning, or at least to comprehend the spirit of the sentiment which my grandfather thought they conveyed.

I cannot help thinking, sir, that if there had been any truth in my grandfather's story, some Scottish member would, on the late occasion, have informed the Chancellor of the Exchequer, that, in virtue of this Treaty, it was no sufficient reason for innovating upon the private rights of Scotsmen in a most tender and delicate point, merely that the Right Honourable Gentleman saw no reason why the same law should not be current through the whole of his Majesty's dominions ; and that, on the contrary, it was incumbent upon him to go a step further, and to show that the alteration proposed *was* for the EVIDENT UTILITY *of the subjects within Scotland,*—a proposition disavowed by the Right Honourable Gentleman's candid admission, as well as by that of the Prime Minister, and contradicted in every circumstance by the actual state of the case.

Methinks, sir, our 'Chosen Five and Forty,' supposing they had bound themselves to Ministers by such oaths of silence and obedience as are taken by Carthusian friars, must have had free-will and speech to express their sentiments, had they been possessed of so irrefragable an argument in such a case of extremity. The sight of a father's life in danger is said to have restored the power of language to the dumb; and truly, the necessary defence of the rights of our native country is not, or at least ought not to be, a less animating motive. Lord Lauderdale almost alone interfered, and procured, to his infinite honour, a delay of six months in the extension of this act,—a sort of reprieve from the southern *jougs*,—by which we may have some chance of profiting, if, during the interval, we can show ourselves true Scotsmen, by some better proof than merely by being 'wise behind the hand.'

In the first place, sir, I would have this old Treaty searched for, and should it be found to be still existing, I think it decides the question. For, how can it be possible that it should be for the 'evident utility' of Scotland to alter her laws of private right, to the total subversion of a system under which she is admitted to have flourished for a century, and which has never within North Britain been attended with the inconveniences charged against it in the sister country, where, by the way, it never existed? Even if the old parchment should be voted obsolete, there would be some satisfaction in having it looked out and pre-served—not in the Register-Office, or Advocates' Library, where it might awaken painful recollections —but in the Museum of the Antiquaries, where, with the Solemn League and Covenant, the Letter of the Scottish Nobles to the Pope on the independence of their country, and other antiquated documents, once held in reverence, it might silently contract dust, yet remain to bear witness that such things had been.

I earnestly hope, however, that an international league of such importance may still be found obligatory on both the *high* and the *low* contracting parties; on that which has the power, and apparently the will, to break it, as well as on the weaker nation, who can-not, without incurring still worse, and more miserable consequences, oppose aggression, otherwise than by invoking the faith of treaties, and the national honour of Old England.

In the second place, all ranks and bodies of men in North Britain (for all are concerned, the poor as well as the rich) should express by petition their sense of the injustice which is offered to the country, and the dis-tress which will probably be the necessary conse-quence. Without the power of issuing their own notes the Banks cannot supply the manufacturer with that credit which enables him to pay his work-men, and wait his return; or accommodate the farmer with that fund which makes it easy for him to discharge his rent, and give wages to his labourers, while in the act of performing expensive operations which are to treble or quadruple the produce of his farm. The trustees on the high-roads and other public works, so ready to stake their personal credit for carrying on public improvements, will no longer possess the power of raising funds by doing so. The whole existing state of credit is to be altered from top to bottom, and Ministers are silent on any remedy which such a state of things would imperiously require.

These are subjects worth struggling for, and rather of more importance than generally come before County Meetings. The English legislature seems inclined to stultify our Law Authorities in their department; but let us at least try if they will listen to the united voice of a Nation in matters which so intimately concern its welfare, that almost every man must have formed a judgment on the subject, from something like personal experience. For my part, I cannot doubt the result.

Times are undoubtedly different from those of Queen Anne, when, Dean Swift having in a political pamphlet passed some sarcasms on the Scottish nation, as a poor and fierce people, the Scythians of Britain,—the Scottish peers, headed by the Duke of Argyll, went in a body to the ministers, and

compelled them to disown the sentiments which had
been expressed by their partisan, and offer a reward
of three hundred pounds for the author of the libel,
well known to be the best advocate and most intimate friend of the existing administration.   They
demanded also that the printer and publisher should
be prosecuted before the House of Peers; and
Harley, however unwillingly, was obliged to yield to
their demand.

In the celebrated case of Porteous, the English
legislature saw themselves compelled to desist from
vindictive measures, on account of a gross offence
committed in the metropolis of Scotland.   In that
of the Roman Catholic bill they yielded to the voice
of the Scottish people, or rather of the Scottish mob,
and declared the proposed alteration of the law
should not extend to North Britain.   The cases were
different, in point of merit, though the Scots were
successful in both.   In the one, a boon of clemency
was extorted; in the other, concession was an act of
decided weakness.   But ought the present administration of Great Britain to show less deference to our
temperate and general remonstrance on a matter
concerning ourselves only, than their predecessors
did to the passions, and even the ill-founded and
unjust prejudices, of our ancestors?

Times, indeed, have changed since those days,
and circumstances also.   We are no longer a poor,

that is, so *very poor* a country and people ; and as we have increased in wealth, we have become somewhat poorer in spirit, and more loath to incur displeasure by contests upon mere etiquette, or national prejudice. But we have some grounds to plead for favour with England. We have borne our pecuniary impositions during a long war, with a patience the more exemplary, as they lay heavier on us from our comparative want of means—our blood has flowed as freely as that of England or of Ireland—our lives and fortunes have become unhesitatingly devoted to the defence of the empire—our loyalty as warmly and willingly displayed towards the person of our Sovereign. We have consented with submission, if not with cheerfulness, to reductions and abolitions of public offices, required for the good of the state at large, but which must affect materially the condition, and even the respectability, of our overburthened aristocracy. We have in every respect conducted ourselves as good and faithful subjects of the general empire.

We do not boast of these things as actual merits ; but they are at least duties discharged, and in an appeal to men of honour and of judgment, must entitle us to be heard with patience, and even deference, on the management of our own affairs, if we speak unanimously, lay aside party feeling, and use the voice of one leaf of the holy Trefoil,—one distinct and component part of the United Kingdoms.

Let no consideration deter us from pleading our own cause temperately but firmly, and we shall certainly receive a favourable audience. Even our acquisition of a little wealth, which might abate our courage on other occasions, should invigorate us to unanimous perseverance at the present crisis, when the very source of our national prosperity is directly, though unwittingly, struck at. Our plaids are, I trust, not yet sunk into Jewish gaberdines, to be wantonly spit upon; nor are we yet bound to 're-ceive the insult with a patient shrug.' But exertion is now demanded on other accounts than those of mere honourable punctilio. Misers themselves will struggle in defence of their property, though tolerant of all aggressions by which that is not threatened. Avarice herself, however mean-spirited, will rouse to defend the wealth she possesses, and preserve the means of gaining more. Scotland is now called upon to rally in defence of the sources of her national improvement, and the means of increasing it; upon which, as none are so much concerned in the subject, none can be such competent judges as Scotsmen themselves.

I cannot believe so generous a people as the English, so wise an administration as the present, will disregard our humble remonstrances, merely because they are made in the form of peaceful entreaty, and not *secundum perfervidum ingenium*

Scotorum, with 'durk and pistol at our belt.' It would be a dangerous lesson to teach the empire at large, that threats can extort what is not yielded to reasonable and respectful remonstrance.

But this is not all. The principle of 'uniformity of laws,' if not manfully withstood, may have other blessings in store for us. Suppose, that when finished with blistering Scotland when in perfect health, England should find time and courage to withdraw the veil from the deep cancer which is gnawing her own bowels, and make an attempt to stop the fatal progress of her *poor-rates.* Some system or other must be proposed in its place—a grinding one it must be, for it is not an evil to be cured by palliatives. Suppose the English, for uniformity's sake, insist that Scotland, which is at present free from this foul and shameful disorder, should nevertheless be included in the severe *treatment* which the disease demands, how would the landholders of Scotland like to undergo the scalpel and cautery, merely because England requires to be scarified?

Or again ;—Supposing England should take a fancy to impart to us her sanguinary criminal code, which, too cruel to be carried into effect, gives every wretch that is condemned a chance of one to twelve that he shall not be executed, and so turns the law into a lottery—would this be an agreeable boon to North Britain?

Once more ;—What if the English ministers should feel disposed to extend to us their equitable system of process respecting civil debt, which divides the advantages so admirably betwixt debtor and creditor—*That* equal dispensation of justice, which provides that an imprisoned debtor, if a rogue, may remain in undisturbed possession of a great landed estate, and enjoy in a jail all the luxuries of Sardanapalus, while the wretch to whom he owes money is starving; and that, to balance the matter, a creditor, if cruel, may detain a debtor in prison for a lifetime, and make, as the established phrase goes, *dice of his bones*—would this admirable reciprocity of privilege, indulged alternately to knave and tyrant, please Saunders better than his own humane action of Cessio, and his equitable process of Adjudication?

I will not insist further on such topics, for I daresay that these apparent enormities in principle are, in England where they have operation, modified and corrected in practice by circumstances unknown to me ; so that, in passing judgment on them, I may myself fall into the error I deprecate, of judging of foreign laws without being aware of all the premisses. Neither do I mean that we should struggle with illiberality against any improvements which can be borrowed from English principle. I would only desire that such ameliorations were adopted, not merely because they are English, but because they are suited to be assimilated with the laws of Scotland, and lead, in short, *to her evident utility*; and this on the principle, that in transplanting a tree, little attention need be paid to the character of the climate and soil from which it is brought, although the greatest care must be taken that those of the situation to which it is transplanted are fitted to receive it. It would be no reason for planting mulberry-trees in Scotland, that they luxuriate in the south of England. There is sense in the old proverb, 'Ilk land has its ain lauch.'

In the present case, it is impossible to believe the extension of these restrictions to Scotland can be for the *evident utility* of the country, which has prospered so long and so uniformly under directly the contrary system.

It is very probable I may be deemed illiberal in all this reasoning; but if to look for information to practical results, rather than to theoretical principles, and to argue from the effect of the experience of a century, rather than the deductions of a modern hypothesis, be illiberal, I must sit down content with a censure, which will include wiser men than I. The philosophical tailors of Laputa, who wrought by mathematical calculation, had, no doubt, a supreme contempt for those humble fashioners who went to work by measuring the person of their customer : but Gulliver tells us, that the worst clothes he ever wore, were constructed upon abstract principles ; and truly, I think, we have seen some laws, and may see more,

U

not much better adapted to existing circumstances, than the Captain's philosophical uniform to his actual person.

It is true, that every wise statesman keeps sound and general political principles in his eye, as the pilot looks upon his compass to discover his true course. But this true course cannot always be followed out straight and diametrically ; it must be altered from time to time, nay sometimes apparently abandoned, on account of shoals, breakers, and headlands, not to mention contrary winds. The same obstacles occur to the course of the statesman. The point at which he aims may be important, the principle on which he steers may be just ; yet the obstacles arising from rooted prejudices, from intemperate passions, from ancient practices, from a different character of people, from varieties in climate and soil, may cause a direct movement upon his ultimate object to be attended with distress to individuals, and loss to the community, which no good man would wish to occasion, and with dangers which no wise man would voluntarily choose to encounter.

Although I think the Chancellor of the Exchequer has been rather precipitate in the decided opinion which he is represented to have expressed on this occasion, I am far from entertaining the slightest disrespect for the right honourable gentleman. 'I hear as good exclamation upon him as on any man in

Messina, and though I am but a poor man, I am glad to hear it.'   But a decided attachment to abstract principle, and to a spirit of generalising, is —like a rash rider on a headstrong horse—very apt to run foul of local obstacles, which might have been avoided by a more deliberate career, where the nature of the ground had been previously considered.

I make allowance for the temptation natural to an ingenious and active mind.   There is a natural pride in following out an universal and levelling principle. It seems to augur genius, force of conception, and steadiness of purpose ; qualities which every legislator is desirous of being thought to possess.   On the other hand, the study of local advantages and impediments demands labour and inquiry, and is rewarded after all only with the cold and parsimonious praise due to humble industry.   It is no less true, however, that measures which go straight and direct to a great general object, without noticing intervening impediments, must often resemble the fierce progress of the thunderbolt or the cannon-ball, those dreadful agents, which, in rushing right to their point, care not what ruin they make by the way.   The sounder and more moderate policy, accommodating its measures to exterior circumstances, rather resembles the judicious course of a well-conducted highway, which, turning aside frequently from its direct course,

' Winds round the corn-field and the hill of vines,'

and becomes devious, that it may respect property and avoid obstacles; thus escaping even temporary evils, and serving the public no less in its more circuitous, than it would have done in its direct course.

Can you tell me, sir, if this *uniformity* of civil institutions, which calls for such sacrifices, be at all descended from, or related to, a doctrine nearly of the same nature, called Conformity in religious doctrine, very fashionable about one hundred and fifty years since, which undertook to unite the jarring creeds of the United Kingdom to one common standard, and excited a universal strife by the vain attempt, and a thousand fierce disputes, in which she

'———umpire sate,
And by decision more embroiled the fray'?

Should Uniformity have the same pedigree, Malachi Malagrowther proclaims her 'a hawk of a very bad nest.'

The universal opinion of a whole kingdom, founded upon a century's experience, ought not to be lightly considered as founded in ignorance and prejudice. I am something of an agriculturist; and in travelling through the country I have often had occasion to wonder that the inhabitants of particular districts had not adopted certain obvious improvements in cultivation. But, upon inquiry, I have usually found out that appearances had deceived me, and that I had not reckoned on particular local circumstances, which either prevented the execution of the system I should have theoretically recommended, or rendered some other more advantageous in the particular circumstances.

I do not therefore resist theoretical innovation in general; I only humbly desire it may not outrun the suggestions arising from the experience of ages. I would have the necessity felt and acknowledged before old institutions are demolished—the *evident utility* of every alteration demonstrated before it is adopted upon mere speculation. I submit our ancient system to the primary knife of the legislature, but would not willingly see our reformers employ a weapon, which, like the sword of Jack the Giant-Killer, *cuts before the point.*

It is always to be considered, that in human affairs, the very best imaginable result is seldom to be obtained, and that it is wise to content ourselves with the best which can be got. This principle speaks with a voice of thunder against violent innovation, for the sake of possible improvement, where things are already well. We ought not to desire better bread than is made of wheat. Our Scotch proverb warns us to *Let weel bide*; and all the world has heard of the untranslatable Italian epitaph upon the man, who died of taking physic to make him better, when he was already in health.—I am, Mr. Journalist, yours,

MALACHI MALAGROWTHER.

Postscript

Since writing these hasty thoughts, I hear it reported that we are to have an extension of our precarious reprieve, and that our six months are to be extended to six years. I would not have Scotland trust to this hollow truce. The measure ought, like all others, to be canvassed on its merits, and frankly admitted or rejected; it has been stirred and ought to be decided. I request my countrymen not to be soothed into inactivity by that temporising, and, I will say, unmanly vacillation. Government is pledged to nothing by taking an open course; for if the bill, so far as applicable to Scotland, is at present absolutely laid aside, there can be no objection to their resuming it at any period, when from change of circumstances, it may be advantageous to Scotland, and when, for what I know, it may be welcomed as a boon.

But if held over our heads as a minatory measure, to take place within a certain period, what can the event be but to cripple and ultimately destroy the present system, on which a direct attack is found at present inexpedient? Can the bankers continue to conduct their profession on the same secure footing, with an abrogation of it in prospect? Must it not cease to be what it has hitherto been—a business carried on both for their own profit, and for the accommodation of the country? Instead of employing their capital in the usual channels, must they not in self-defence employ it in forming others? Will not the substantial and wealthy withdraw their funds from that species of commerce? And may not the place of these be supplied by men of daring adventure, without corresponding capital, who will take a chance of wealth or ruin in the chances of the game?

If it is the absolute and irrevocable determination that the bill is to be extended to us, the sooner the great penalty is inflicted the better; for in politics and commerce, as in all the other affairs of life, absolute and certain evil is better than uncertainty and protracted suspense.

NOTES

P. 3.

The exclusion—of James from the succession.
The rebellion—Monmouth's.

P. 6.

The Quakers.—A hit, of course, at Penn.

P. 17.

Piqueer, 'do outpost duty,' 'raid.'

P. 18.

Lords of the Articles.—A well-known body in the older Scottish Constitution, through whom only legislation could be originated, and who thus almost nullified the powers of Parliament.

P. 20.

Squeaziness = 'squeamishness,' 'queasiness.'

It is impossible.—Another form of ' No bishop no king.'

The new converts. — After the Revocation of the Edict of Nantes.

P. 22.

T. W. is, of course, a mere fancy signature. It might stand for ' True Wellwisher' or anything. The wiseacres took it as = ' W. T.,' William Temple.

P. 27.

Neither, for ' too,' is colloquial but rather picturesque. Cf. the famous ' And yet but yaw neither' in *Hamlet*.

P. 47.

I have not thought it desirable to reproduce the abundance of italics with which the original is furnished. They no doubt appealed to the vulgar, as where poor Mr. Wood is described (p. 50) as ' *a mean ordinary man, a hardware dealer.*' But the vigour of the onslaught is wholly independent of them.

P. 50.

Written—by Swift himself.

P. 54.

Bere, or ' bear,' also ' bigg,' a kind of barley largely culti-vated in Ireland, Scotland, and Northern England. It has six rows in the ear, and will grow in much poorer ground and a much damper and rougher climate than the two-rowed variety. It is also, I believe, still thought to give the best whisky, if not the best beer, when malted.

P. 55.

Conolly—Speaker of the Irish House of Commons.

P. 56.

Pistole—about ten shillings.

P. 60.

Brought to the bullion seems here to have the meaning of the French *billonner* or *envoyer au billon*, ' to melt for recoining.'

P. 74.

Our Cæsar's statue.—The statue of George I. on Essex Bridge, Dublin.

P. 89.

Contignation.—This rather pedantic, and now, I think, quite obsolete word (from *tignum*, ' beam ') means ' having a common or continuous roof.'

P. 99.

The slackness of England in taking advantage of the Vendéan and Chouan movements, of which Burke here complains, has never been fully explained. The poltroonery of the Bourbon princes, and the factions of the emigrants, throw a certain but not a complete light on it ; and though conjectural explanations are obvious enough, there is little positive evidence to support them.

P. 107.

But when the possibility . . . that the.—It will probably seem to a modern reader that either 'that' or 'the' has crept in improperly. It might be so; but Burke still maintained the authoritative but rather inelegant tradition by which 'that,' like the French *que*, could replace any such antecedent word as 'when,' 'because,' etc.

P. 112.

Louis the Sixteenth.—To this is appended a note in the editions beginning, 'It may be right to do justice to Louis XVI.   He did what he could to destroy the double diplomacy of France.'   The subject has of late years received considerable illustration in the Duke of Broglie's *Le Secret du Roi*, and other works by the same author.

P. 114.

Montalembert.—Marc René, Marquis de (1714-1800), a voluminous military writer.

P. 124.

Harrington—of the *Oceana.*

P. 134.

Dear Abraham.—'Peter Plymley' addresses his *Letters* to 'my brother Abraham, who lives in the country,' and is a parson.

P. 136.

Baron Maseres.—Cursitor Baron of the Exchequer, a descendant of Huguenots, very well thought of by his contemporaries.   Dr. Rennel I know not, unless he was the Herodotus man.

P. 137.

C——, Canning.

P. 138.

Dr. Duigenan.—A delightful person who, in his hot youth, as a junior Fellow of T. C., D., threatened to 'bulge the Provost's' [Provost Hely Hutchinson's] 'eye,' and was afterwards a pillar of Protestantism.

P. 144.

This *light and frivolous jester* was *not* the Rev. Sydney Smith, but George Canning, Esq.

P. 154.

The pecuniary Rose.—'Old George' Rose, Pitt's right hand. He was rather heavily rewarded with places and pensions ; but even Liberals now admit that the country has hardly had an abler official.

Lord Hawkesbury, Jenkinson, better known as Lord Liverpool.

P. 157.

Tickell—the *Rolliad* Tickell.

P. 170.

Joel—Peter's nephew and Abraham's son.

P. 193.

Paint in the most horrid colours.—See, for instance, *The Bloody Buoy* and *The Cannibal's Progress*, by William Cobbett.

P. 225.

Flogging.—Some of the militia mutinied at Ely, and were punished, the guard on the occasion being furnished by the cavalry of the German Legion. Cobbett noticed this in the most inflammatory manner, and it being war time, was indicted, tried, found guilty, and sentenced as he describes.

P. 229.

Monks and friars.—A time came when Cobbett thought and wrote very differently of these persons. But that was his way.

P. 245.

Foundal.—I do not know whether Cobbett invented this equivalent for *trouvaille,* 'windfall,' or not. His notable scheme for breaking the Bank is a good example of him in his insaner moods.

P. 253.

The Duenna—Sheridan's.

P. 256.

The Jury Court.—Trial by jury in *civil* cases was only introduced into Scotland in 1815.

P. 259.

Evasive answer—to the effect that each queen was the fairest woman in her own country.

P. 272.

Doer = 'factor' or agent.

P. 277.

Them—as if 'Scotsmen' had been written for 'Scotland.'

P. 281.

Chosen Five and Forty—the original number of members assigned to Scotland.

P. 283.

Political pamphlet—'The Public Spirit of the Whigs.'

P. 287.

Durk, sic in original.

P. 288.

Cessio, sc. bonorum, whereby a debtor on giving up his property could be relieved of liabilities.

Adjudication, whereby a creditor could attach landed as well as personal property.

P. 289.

Lauch = 'laugh.'

Printed by R. & R. CLARK, *Edinburgh.*